let's talk type

D0995518

First published in the United Kingdom in 2016
by Thames & Hudson Ltd.
181A High Holborn, London WC1V 7QX

Copyright © 2016 RotoVision SA

Publisher: Mark Searle
Editorial Director: Isheeta Mustafi
Commissioning Editor: Alison Morris
Editor: Nick Jones
Assistant Editor: Abbie Sharman
Creative Direction: Agata Rybicka
Design: Tony Seddon
Cover Design: Agata Rybicka

British Library Cataloguing-in-Publication Data
A catalogue record for this book is available from the British Library.

ISBN: 978-0-500-29229-7

Printed and bound in China

To find out about all our publications, please visit
www.thamesandhudson.com. There you can subscribe
to our e-newsletter, browse or download our current
catalogue, and buy any titles that are in print.

Front cover design based on Herb Lubalin's 1959 poster 'Let's Talk Type, Let Type Talk'.
Used here with kind permission from The Herb Lubalin Study Centre of Design and Typography, New York.

Title set in Domaine Display Black.

Trademarks
Adobe Typekit, InDesign, OpenType and PostScript ® are registered trademarks of Adobe Systems Incorporated
in the United States and/ or other countries.
Mac and OS X are trademarks of Apple Inc., registered in the United States and other countries.

TONY SEDDON

let's talk type

an essential lexicon
of type terms ●●●

Thames & Hudson

!	Exclamation point p37	**&**	Ampersand p44	**b b**	Character p52	**H**	Hairline p59
?	Question mark p37	**#**	Octothorpe p44	**Nhg**	Metrics p53	**o!**	Boldface p60
" "	Quotes p38	**@**	@ symbol p45	**ono**	Sidebearing p53	**U.**	Novelty type p60
''	Primes p38	**©**	Copyright p45	ABCDEFG HIJKLMN OPQRSTU VWXYZ	Uppercase p54	**a**	Single-storey p61
( )	Parentheses p39	**★**	Asterisk p46	abcdefg hijklmn opqrstu vwxyz	Lowercase p54	**a**	Double-storey p61
¶	Pilcrow p39	**●**	Bullet p46	AaBbCcDdEe FfGgHhIiJjKk LlMmNnOoPp QqRrSsTtUu VvWwXxYyZz	Bicameral p55	**Ge**	Calligraphic p62
—	Hyphen p40	**† †**	Dagger p47	abcdef ghijklm nopqrst uvwxyz	Unicameral p55	**Q**	Swash Character p62
—	Dash p40	**☞**	Manicule p47	**rome**	Roman p56	**G**	Inline font p63
• • •	Ellipsis p41	CHAPTER 3 Type Terms		*i i*	Italic p56	**C**	Chromatic type p63
o	Degree p41	**g**	Typeface p50	*gg*	Oblique roman p57	**m**	Condensed p64
g	Glyph p42	**g**	Font p50	**k**	Back slant p57	**m**	Compressed p64
�֍	Dingbat p42	Gill Sans Gill Sans Gill Sans **Gill Sans** **Gill Sans**	Weight p51	*Ol*	Slope p58	**m**	Expanded p65
fi	Ligature p43	*Bembo* **Bembo** ***Bembo*** **Bembo**	Style p51	Text Caption Subhead Display	Optical sizes p58	Lorem ipsum dolo adipiscing elit, sed euismod tincidunt aliquam erat volut minim veniam, qu ullamcorper suscip	Colour p65
‽	Interrobang p43	ABCDEFGHI JKLMNOPQR STUVWXYZ abcdefghijklmn opqrstuvwxyz	Alphabet p52	**C**	Contrast p59	≡≡≡≡	Alignment p66

A TIMELINE OF TYPE

Johannes Gutenberg is credited with the earliest successful use of movable type in the late 1440s. Since then, typeface design has clearly not stood still, and a number of different classifications of type now exist. This timeline provides a broad overview of the periods during which each recognised classification of typeface *first appeared*. A more detailed explanation of each classification can be found in chapter 4, which starts on page 86.

**ANCIENT
(PRE-VENETIAN)**
Pre-fifteenth century

**BLACKLETTER
(TEXTURA or FRAKTUR)**
Mid-fifteenth century

**HUMANIST SERIF
(VENETIAN)**
Late fifteenth century

**OLD STYLE SERIF
(GARALDE)**
Sixteenth century

TRANSITIONAL SERIF
Eighteenth century

**RATIONAL SERIF
(DIDONE or MODERN)**
Late eighteenth century

SCRIPT
Late eighteenth century

GROTESQUE SANS SERIF
Early nineteenth century

DISPLAY
Early nineteenth century

**SLAB SERIF
(CLARENDON)**
Mid-nineteenth century

**GOTHIC, GEOMETRIC,
and HUMANIST
SANS SERIF**
Early twentieth century

NEO-GROTESQUE SANS
Mid-twentieth century

NEO-HUMANIST SANS
Late twentieth century

CONTEMPORARY SERIF
Late twentieth century

INTRODUCTION

Becoming a type nerd can be something of an occupational hazard when you're a graphic designer. This doesn't always happen of course; some designers are happy to quietly ply their trade without feeling the need to debate the virtues of Avenir in comparison with Futura (are there any?), or why oldstyle figures are better than lining figures in running text (but are they?). However, if you're someone who does enjoy a lively discussion about the decline in the use of the pilcrow, or whether true italics trump a well-designed oblique roman, this could be just the book you need if you're to avoid an embarrassing typographic *faux pas*.

During the last 460 or so years, typography and typesetting have garnered a rich collection of terms and definitions, many of which draw from the earliest practices when individual glyphs (or sorts) were cut, cast and composed into blocks of text entirely by hand. For example, we still talk about leading (see page 69) when we talk about line spacing, despite the fact that metal type began to fall out of commercial use during the 1960s with the advent of phototypesetting. All the key terms are included and illustrated in the first three sections of this book; *The Anatomy of Type*, *Glyphs* and the all-important *Type Terms* chapter.

There are a couple of important points to highlight at this juncture. Firstly, the type classifications I describe in chapter 4 are based largely on the Vox-ATypI system devised by the French historian Maximilien Vox in 1954. It's generally accepted that this pre-digital system has become somewhat out-of-date during the last thirty years, but it still works well for the majority of classic typefaces. The principal difference introduced here is the use of the broadened 'Rational' classification (see page 90), which includes Didones, typefaces that appear to be constructed rather than written.

In the final section, *The Typefaces*, we look at forty-three individual typefaces, grouped by classification and ordered by the year in which they *first appeared* as either movable type, phototype or as a digital font. Many of the classic typefaces we use today (such as Jenson or Bembo) are based closely on letterforms created as far back as the fifteenth century and their names are contemporary contrivances drawn from their origins – it's those origins which dictate the running order here. The key characters of each typeface appear in red to help you identify them. Also, we illustrate as many weights and styles for each typeface as room allows, but many of the faces contain additional fonts that you can research and purchase from good online retailers such as MyFonts and fonts.com, or from subscription-based sources such as Adobe Typekit.

I hope this book helps to arm you with all the information you may need if you happen to find yourself embroiled in a conversation about type. It certainly helped to clear up a couple of grey areas for me while I was writing it!

Tony Seddon

Chapter 1

Type Anatomy

X-HEIGHT

The height of the **lowercase** 'x' of any given typeface. The 'x' is used for this measurement because it has no **ascenders** or **descenders**, and because it has no round forms that sit below the **baseline**.

The x-height is an important identifier for any given typeface and it's generally accepted that typefaces with a large x-height are more legible, particularly when used at either small text or large display point sizes.

» LOWERCASE – SEE PAGE 54
» ASCENDER – SEE PAGE 16
» DESCENDER – SEE PAGE 16
» BASELINE – SEE BELOW

BASELINE

The invisible line that demarcates the point at which all glyphs of a typeface sit. Note that the bases of rounded glyphs generally dip slightly below the baseline, as do the **descenders**.

There are few exceptions to the rules when it comes to the positioning of characters on a baseline, but some casual script typefaces use a variable alignment to create a 'handwritten' feeling. **Suomi Hand Script** is a good example of a font that does this.

» DESCENDER – SEE PAGE 16
» SUOMI HAND SCRIPT – SEE PAGE 142

ASCENDER LINE

The invisible demarcation line that marks the uppermost reach of the ascenders in any one typeface or font. Note that this is often slightly higher than the maximum height of the **uppercase** glyphs, as shown by the paler 'I' overlaying the **lowercase** 'h' to the right. The ratio between the **x-height** and the length of ascenders provides an important visual characteristic for a typeface, and can aid identification. For example, Old Style Serifs like **Garamond** have a low x-height and relatively tall ascenders.

» Uppercase – see page 54
» Lowercase – see page 54
» X-height – see page 12
» Garamond – see page 104

CAP HEIGHT

The invisible demarcation line that marks the uppermost reach of the uppercase glyphs in any one typeface or font. Note that this is often slightly lower than the maximum height of the **ascenders,** as shown by the paler 'h' overlaying the uppercase 'I' to the right. Not all typefaces exhibit this characteristic, and the difference between cap height and ascender length isn't an attribute that can realistically be used for font identification, but the small difference in height can create a perceptible variation in **body** height which may produce text setting with a somewhat livelier appearance.

» Ascender – see page 16
» Body – see page 32

APEX

The uppermost junction at which two **strokes** meet to form an angle of less than 90 degrees. As well as the example illustrated to the right, this could be the central junction of a 'W'. The width of an apex, i.e. the 'flat' part of the join, is usually governed by the width of either the thickest or thinnest stroke. In our example (Adobe **Jenson**) the thinnest stroke provides the width of the apex. Some typefaces such as **Bembo** (below right) have a small projection at the apex, which can aid identification. The term is derived from the Latin *apex*, meaning summit or peak.

» STROKE – SEE PAGE 24
» JENSON – SEE PAGE 100
» BEMBO – SEE PAGE 102

VERTEX

The lowermost **joint** at which two **stems** meet to form an angle of less than 90 degrees. As well as the example illustrated to the right, this could be the central junction of an 'M'. The width of a vertex is usually governed by the width of either the thickest or thinnest stroke. In our example (Adobe **Jenson**) the thinnest stroke provides the width of the vertex. A narrow vertex usually produces more of an **overshoot** than a flatter join.

» JOINT – SEE PAGE 32
» STEM – SEE PAGE 17
» JENSON – SEE PAGE 100
» OVERSHOOT – SEE PAGE 15

OVERSHOOT

The portion of a **vertex** that dips below the **baseline** in some typefaces. When present they provide a degree of optical compensation, helping to anchor wide characters to the baseline, and can be difficult to detect at small point sizes. It should be noted that very prominent overshoots (as with **Futura** for example) can be visually distracting at much larger point sizes. This is something to bear in mind when selecting a face for display use.

» VERTEX – SEE PAGE 14
» BASELINE – SEE PAGE 12
» FUTURA – SEE PAGE 152

CROTCH

The space formed at the **joint** of two strokes, or where an arch meets a stem. Crotches can be greater than 90 degrees (obtuse) or smaller than 90 degrees (acute) in characters such as the 'w' illustrated here, and form a right angle at the inner corners of characters such as the 'F' or 'E'. The angle naturally decreases for narrow characters such as those in a condensed face. Typeface designers sometimes compensate for this by using devices such as a lower degree of contrast in typefaces with a narrow overall width, thus producing a flatter, wider **apex** or **vertex**.

» JOINT – SEE PAGE 32
» APEX – SEE PAGE 14
» VERTEX – SEE PAGE 14

ASCENDER (EXTENDER)

The vertical **stem** of a lowercase **glyph** which travels upwards above the **x-height**. As well as the illustrated example, this could be the upper portion of a 'b', 'h' or 'k'. Ascenders can also be referred to generically as extenders.

Tall ascenders can add a sense of grace and history to a typeface; for example, the early twentieth century saw a trend for typefaces with tall extenders combined with a fairly low x-height.

» STEM – SEE PAGE 17
» GLYPH – SEE PAGE 42
» X-HEIGHT – SEE PAGE 12

DESCENDER (EXTENDER)

The vertical stem of a **lowercase** glyph which travels down toward (and beyond) the **baseline**. As well as the illustrated example, this could be the lower portion of a 'j' or 'q'. **Descenders** can also be referred to generically as extenders.

Typefaces with long descenders should be avoided if vertical space is at a premium, thus creating the need for tight **leading**, as this may result in ascenders or descenders clashing with adjacent lines of type.

» LOWERCASE – SEE PAGE 54
» BASELINE – SEE PAGE 12
» LEADING – SEE PAGE 69

STEM

The main vertical **stroke** or strokes of a **glyph**. Stems are sometimes referred to as a 'vertical stroke', and generally represent the thickest stroke or strokes of any given character. Straight but angled strokes, such as those that form the sides of the uppercase 'A' or 'V', can also be considered as stems.

» Stroke – see page 24
» Glyph – see page 42

LEG

The downward **stroke**, commonly but not exclusively a diagonal, which appears in the lower portion of characters such as the 'K' and 'R'.

Some typefaces, for example **Bembo**, feature a very long leg on the 'R', which extends far into the **body** of adjacent characters, creating spacing issues. To combat this, some contemporary digital releases of faces where this occurs are supplied with an alternative glyph featuring a shorter leg, thus alleviating the spacing problems.

» Stroke – see page 24
» Bembo – see page 102
» Body – see page 32

ARM

A **stroke** that can extend either horizontally or diagonally from a vertical stem. As well as the example illustrated here, this could be the upward travelling diagonal stroke of an uppercase 'K'. The **uppercase** 'E' can be useful for identifying a serif's classification. **Humanist** and **Old Style** serifs tend to have a fairly long central arm, while **Transitional** and **Rational** serifs often feature a central arm which is distinctly shorter.

» STROKE – SEE PAGE 24
» UPPERCASE – SEE PAGE 54
» HUMANIST SERIF – SEE PAGE 89
» OLD STYLE SERIF – SEE PAGE 89
» TRANSITIONAL SERIF – SEE PAGE 90
» RATIONAL SERIF – SEE PAGE 90

CROSSBAR (BAR)

The particular kind of **cross stroke** that joins the two vertical **stems** of an uppercase 'A' or 'H'. The term 'Bar' can be interchangeable with 'Crossbar'.

More often than not, the crossbar of an 'H' will be close to the mid-line so it aligns with the central **arm** of the 'E', but occasionally it's drawn slightly higher to provide visual balance. Characters with a lower half that's visually larger can appear more stable on the baseline.

» CROSS STROKE – SEE PAGE 19
» STEM – SEE PAGE 17
» ARM – SEE ABOVE

CROSS STROKE

The generally asymmetric horizontal stroke that crosses the stem of the **lowercase** characters 'f' and 't'. As shown in the illustration to the right, cross strokes in Humanist, Old Style and Transitional serifs are joined to the left of the ascender or stem by a short diagonal stroke, providing an identifying characteristic. This characteristic is missing from Rational Serifs and sans serif faces.

Cross strokes should not be confused with **arms** or **crossbars** as the latter join with stems but do not cross them.

» LOWERCASE – SEE PAGE 54
» ARM – SEE PAGE 18
» CROSSBAR – SEE PAGE 18

WAIST

The point where the upper and lower **bowls** (or **lobes**) of an **uppercase** 'B' meet. For optical balance the waist is often placed slightly above the vertical centre of the character.

The waist plays an important role in determining how wide a character can be. To maintain the proportions of the lobes as described above, the waist must be raised slightly if a character's width is increased (say in the case of an expanded weight introduced as part of a larger **family**).

» BOWL – SEE PAGE 20
» LOBE – SEE PAGE 21
» UPPERCASE – SEE PAGE 54
» FAMILY – SEE PAGE 85

BOWL

The curved stroke which encloses the round portion of characters such as the lowercase 'a' or uppercase 'B'. Bowls can be fully enclosed, as per our illustrated example to the right, or open. An open bowl doesn't connect fully with the stem – **Garamond**'s uppercase 'P' provides an example.

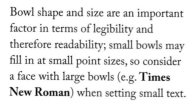

Bowl shape and size are an important factor in terms of legibility and therefore readability; small bowls may fill in at small point sizes, so consider a face with large bowls (e.g. **Times New Roman**) when setting small text.

» GARAMOND – SEE PAGE 104
» TIMES NEW ROMAN – SEE PAGE 122

SHOULDER

A curved **stroke** extending outwards and downwards from the top of a **stem**, often joining another stem to form the upper portion of a **leg**. The **lowercase** 'h', 'm' and 'n' all contain shoulders.

Even in sans serif faces, where stroke contrast is generally lower than it is in serif faces, the shoulder is nearly always tapered to its thinnest width at the point where it meets the vertical stem, thus avoiding the problem of 'ink trap', where the upper notch fills in during printing.

» STROKE – SEE PAGE 24
» STEM – SEE PAGE 17
» LEG – SEE PAGE 17
» LOWERCASE – SEE PAGE 54

LOOP

A **counter**, often closed, that extends below the **baseline** and connects to an upper counter via a **link**. The **lowercase** 'g' contains a loop when it appears in binocular, or **double-storey**, form. Loops can be asymmetrical, meaning that the thinnest part of the stroke may be angled, even in characters with an upright **stress**. An open loop (as in **Baskerville** for example) provides a key identifier for a typeface.

» Counter – see page 31
» Baseline – see page 12
» Link – see page 23
» Lowercase – see page 54
» Double-storey – see page 61
» Stress – see page 24
» Baskerville – see page 108

LOBES

The upper and lower **bowls** of an **uppercase** 'B'. Technically these portions could also be referred to as bowls or **strokes**. To achieve optical balance, the lower lobe of a 'B' is almost always larger than the upper lobe; if the lobes were equal in size the character would appear to be set upside down.

» Bowl – see page 20
» Uppercase – see page 54
» Stroke – see page 24

ARC OF STEM

A curved stroke that seamlessly continues from a vertical or horizontal **stem**. This could be seen as an alternative definition for the term 'tail' when applied to certain characters such as the 'J' and is also sometimes referred to as a descending **hook**. Generally speaking there are two types of hook shape for a 'j'; it can be short and narrow so it fits within the body of the **character**, or it can curve to the left so it extends below an adjacent **glyph**. Many Rational and Slab Serif faces feature a hook with a ball terminal.

» STEM – SEE PAGE 17
» HOOK – SEE BELOW
» CHARACTER – SEE PAGE 52
» GLYPH – SEE PAGE 42

HOOK (ARCH)

A curved **stroke** that extends upwards from a **stem** but terminates before it begins to form a **bowl**. The form of the hook is particularly important for the lowercase 'f', and it often mirrors the shape of the descending hook of the lowercase 'j'. A narrow hook which doesn't extend to the right will make letterspacing simpler but it may in turn reduce legibility (the 'f' will be closer in appearance to the 't'). It's for this reason that **ligatures** such as 'fi' and 'fl' are so useful.

» STROKE – SEE PAGE 24
» STEM – SEE PAGE 17
» BOWL – SEE PAGE 20
» LIGATURE – SEE PAGE 43

LINK

The short **stroke** that connects the upper and lower **bowls** of a 'g' when it appears in a binocular, or **double-storey**, form. In typefaces with a large degree of **contrast**, the link transitions from its narrowest stroke width at its topmost point to the widest at its base. Humanist Serif and Old Style Serif faces generally feature a link that transitions abruptly to the left, reflecting the calligraphic structures of these classifications. The links of Transitional and Slab Serif faces are more constructed and curve more gracefully to meet the lower bowl.

» STROKE – SEE PAGE 24
» BOWL – SEE PAGE 20
» DOUBLE-STOREY – SEE PAGE 61
» CONTRAST – SEE PAGE 59

TAIL

Commonly, a descending **stroke** on characters such as the **uppercase** 'Q' or at the terminal of the **leg** of the uppercase 'R'. For the **lowercase** 'g', 'j' and 'y', the stroke that extends below the **baseline** can also be called a tail. The method used to join the tail to the counter provides a key identifier; for example **Clarendon** has a tail which curves upwards into the counter before extending to the right with a vertical flick.

» STROKE – SEE PAGE 24
» UPPERCASE – SEE PAGE 54
» LEG – SEE PAGE 17
» LOWERCASE – SEE PAGE 54
» BASELINE – SEE PAGE 12
» CLARENDON – SEE PAGE 130

AXIS (STRESS)

The invisible line that indicates the angle of stress of a typeface or font. This angle varies from typeface to typeface and can be ascertained by drawing a line between the two thinnest points of the round stroke of the uppercase 'O'. Axes are generally backward leaning but some faces do feature a forward leaning axis. The Humanist Sans typeface Syntax provides us with an example of this.

The angle of stress can be useful for identifying a serif's classification. Humanist serifs are steeply angled, Old Styles tend to be less so, while Transitionals, Rationals and most sans serifs have an upright stress.

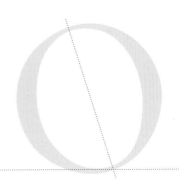

STROKE

The straight or curved components of any **glyph** that are neither vertical nor horizontal. **Stems** are sometimes referred to as a 'vertical stroke', while **crossbars** are sometimes referred to as a 'horizontal stroke'. The relative width of all strokes, from thinnest to thickest, provides us with a description of a typeface's **contrast**.

» Glyph – see page 42
» Stem – see page 17
» Crossbar – see page 18
» Contrast – see page 59

SWASH

The ornamental extension added to a standard **stroke**, particularly for **italic** styles, with the intention of creating a more flamboyant personality for typography. Swashes are sometimes also referred to as **finials**, especially if they're significantly tapered.

» Stroke – see page 24
» Italic – see page 56
» Finial – see page 27

SPINE

The curved **stroke** that forms the central portion of the **uppercase** and **lowercase** 'S'. Curvature can vary considerably between typefaces, with some spines appearing much flatter in faces with a wider character width; classic Neo-Grotesque Sans Serif faces such as **Univers** or **Helvetica** provide examples of this 'look'.

In typefaces with a high degree of contrast the central portion of the spine is normally the point where the stroke is thickest.

» Stroke – see page 24
» Uppercase – see page 54
» Lowercase – see page 54
» Univers – see page 160
» Helvetica – see page 162

EAR

The small projection that arises on the top right side of the upper **bowl** of the **lowercase** 'g' when it appears in its binocular form, as illustrated to the right. The ear shouldn't be confused with a **beak** – beaks are an extension of a stroke that extends beyond an adjoining stroke.

The ear is normally positioned at the same level as the **x-height**, and tends not to extend too far to the right in order to avoid letterspacing issues.

» Bowl – see page 20
» Lowercase – see page 54
» Beak – see below
» X-height – see page 12

BEAK

The small projection that extends beyond an adjoining **stroke**, or forms a sharp **terminal** at the end of an arch. They occur commonly in, for example, Humanist Serif faces like **Jenson** (see right) with their calligraphic influence, and reflect the way the pen stroke would have continued past the join of a straight and a curved stroke if the character were hand-lettered.

A beak shouldn't be confused with an **ear** – ears are an individual stroke which is attached to a **bowl**, rather than an extension.

» Stroke – see page 24
» Terminal – see page 100
» Jenson – see page 29
» Ear – see above
» Bowl – see page 20

FINIAL

A tapered **terminal** which finishes a **stroke**, **arch** or **crossbar**, as illustrated to the right. They occur commonly across a wide range of typefaces, particularly serif faces with the noticeable degree of **contrast** necessary to produce a tapered stroke, and are too commonplace to aid with font identification. Ornamental flourishes and **swashes** are also referred to as finials.

» TERMINAL – SEE PAGE 29
» STROKE – SEE PAGE 24
» ARCH – SEE PAGE 22
» CROSSBAR – SEE PAGE 18
» CONTRAST – SEE PAGE 59
» SWASH – SEE PAGE 25

SPUR

Any small, sharp projection that extends from a **stroke** or **stem**. Spurs often appear at **terminals** but can also be added at joints where a circular stroke meets a stem, as with an uppercase 'G'. Look at a sample of the Old Style typeface Galliard for a prominent example of a spur of this variety. Old Style and Transitional Serif faces commonly feature spurs in their character sets.

» STROKE – SEE PAGE 24
» STEM – SEE PAGE 17
» TERMINAL – SEE PAGE 29

DOT (TITTLE)

Simply the dot above the **lowercase** 'i' and 'j'. The alternative name 'tittle' is rarely used nowadays, and technically the dot can also be referred to as a *superscript* dot. If a **diacritic** appears above the 'i' or 'j', or if either character is combined as a **ligature**, the dot is generally omitted.

Dots vary in shape between typefaces; they can be circular, square or diamond shaped. Circular and diamond shaped dots are usually slightly wider than the stem, while square dots generally match the stem's width.

» Lowercase – see page 54
» Diacritic – see below
» Ligature – see page 43

DIACRITIC (ACCENT)

A mark added to a glyph (which can be both **uppercase** and **lowercase**) that gives it a specific phonetic value. Commonly seen examples are the umlaut (dieresis or trema) illustrated to the right, the acute accent 'é', the grave accent 'è', the circumflex 'ê' and the cedilla 'ç'. Some typefaces feature a limited range of diacritics, so take care to check this if you're setting text in a language requiring them, for example, French or German.

Diacritics are also commonly referred to as accents or accent marks outside of typographic terminology.

» Uppercase – see page 54
» Lowercase – see page 54

TERMINAL

The end of a **stem** or **stroke**. The terminals of different serif typefaces can vary in shape; for example an overtly tapered terminal can be called a **finial**, while a ball terminal ends with a pronounced circular form. The examples below show Joanna's tapered finial, and Archer's ball terminal.

» STEM – SEE PAGE 17
» STROKE – SEE PAGE 24
» FINIAL – SEE PAGE 27

Tapered terminal (or finial)   Ball terminal

GADZOOK (QUAINT)

An antiquated term for a particular style of embellishment connecting two letterforms to form a discretionary **ligature** intended to provide a degree of historical flavour to a piece of typesetting. There's no particular functionality attached to these ornamental additions beyond their decorative qualities, so it's advisable to use them only in connection with appropriate subject matter.

» LIGATURE – SEE PAGE 43

APERTURE

The opening that delineates the interior and exterior areas of a **glyph** with an **open counter**. This term can also be applied to the area fully enclosed by the strokes of the glyph.

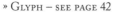

Larger, open apertures can help to improve legibility, particularly when glyphs are viewed on a screen. For example, during rapid reading a 'c' with a large aperture looks less like an 'o', or an 'e' less like an 'a'. Aperture size is a key element for designers to consider when creating a typeface for a specific function, for example a face intended primarily for the screen.

» Glyph – see page 42
» Open counter – see page 31

EYE

The closed **bowl** in the topmost portion of a **lowercase** 'e'. Technically the eye could also be referred to as a **closed counter**, but traditionally this term has long been associated with this character.

Similarly to **bowls**, the shape and size of the eye are important factors in terms of legibility and therefore readability; small eyes may fill-in at small point sizes, so look for a face with open eyes (e.g. **News Gothic**) for very small text.

» Bowl – see page 20
» Lowercase – see page 54
» Counter (closed) – see page 31
» News Gothic – see page 150

COUNTER (CLOSED)

The fully enclosed area within characters such as 'a', 'b', 'd', 'g', 'o', 'p' and 'q'.

Large counters, which by default tend to produce a large **x-height**, can help to improve legibility because they aid character recognition. It's generally accepted that larger proportions in **lowercase** characters improves legibility and readability. Some sources may also refer to counters as **bowls**.

» X-HEIGHT – SEE PAGE 12
» LOWERCASE – SEE PAGE 54
» BOWL – SEE PAGE 20

COUNTER (OPEN)

The partially enclosed area within characters such as 'h', 'm', 'n', 's', 'u', 'v', 'w', 'x', 'y' and 'z'. The use of the term counter can cause confusion because they don't have to be round; any area of empty space within a glyph can be a counter. Open counters are also sometimes referred to as **apertures**.

As mentioned above, it's generally accepted that larger counters in **lowercase** characters improve legibility and readability due to the increased ease of character recognition.

» APERTURE – SEE PAGE 30
» LOWERCASE – SEE PAGE 54

BODY

Essentially the point size of a typeface or font, the body is the area populated by each of the glyphs of a font; with the height of the body providing the said point size. The term originates from the days of handset foundry type when each glyph sat on the end of an individual slug of metal called a **sort**.

» Glyph (Sort) – see page 42

JOINT

The junction formed when a **stroke** meets a **stem**. Joints can be right angled, less than 90 degrees (acute) or more than 90 degrees (obtuse). The example shown to the right is a typical 90 degree joint where a stem meets an arm; acute or obtuse angled joints occur where stems or strokes meet to form a **crotch**.

» Stroke – see page 24
» Stem – see page 17
» Crotch – see page 15

BRACKET

The portion of a **serif** which transitions smoothly outwards from the stem in an unbroken curve or angled wedge. The style of bracket is normally expressed as part of the term used to describe the serif itself. The three principal styles of serif are illustrated in the entry below.

Brackets are always a useful feature to look at when identifying a typeface's classification. For example, Humanist Serifs and Old Style Serifs often feature a gradual curve to the bracket, a Transitional Serif's bracket will be more abrupt and engineered, and a Contemporary Serif may have wedge serifs or even a mix of all the above.

» Serif – see below

SERIF

The small strokes that appear at the terminus of stems, arms, **ascenders** and **descenders** in a serif typeface. There are three main types of serif; bracketed serifs merge into strokes with a smooth curve, wedge serifs transform into the stroke using an angled slope, and unbracketed serifs join at an abrupt 90 degree angle.

Humanist, Old Style and Transitional Serif faces are bracketed; Rationals (generally) and Slabs have unbracketed serifs, while wedge serifs often appear in Contemporary Serif faces.

» Ascender – see page 16
» Descender – see page 16

Bracketed serif   Wedge serif   Unbracketed serif

Chapter 2

Glyphs

FULL POINT (PERIOD)

Called variously a full point, a period (in North America) or a full stop, this glyph does more than simply finish sentences. It can also succeed a shortened initial in someone's name, indicate an abbreviated word or carry several mathematical contexts including the decimal point. The glyph can be circular, square or even diamond shaped.

Typographic convention indicates that a single space should be used after a full point, not a double space. The use of a double space harks back to the era of typewriters and their monospaced typefaces, where a single space after a full point was harder to spot.

COMMA

Principally, the humble comma performs the vital role of punctuating a sentence so it can be read at the correct pace. The word derives from the Greek *komma*, which can be interpreted to mean 'a short clause'. The comma is also used as a decimal point throughout Europe, rather than the full point used in North America and Britain.

Commas always sit on the baseline, and can appear as either a straight angled mark or in the classic 'filled-in number 9' form with a round or square dot. In some Eastern European languages the comma can also be combined with characters as a **diacritic**.

» Diacritic – see page 28

EXCLAMATION POINT (MARK)

Historically, the exclamation point, or exclamation mark, was also rather marvellously known to printers as a screamer or a bang. Its principal use is obvious; it indicates a loud exclamation when placed at the end of a phrase or sentence. In Spanish, an additional inverted exclamation mark is also placed at the beginning of the phrase.

Its origins are thought to be medieval Latin, where the word *io* meaning 'hurrah' was written at the end of a sentence to indicate joy. Over time the 'i' moved above the 'o' to form the symbol. Graphically it is recognised internationally as a warning.

QUESTION MARK

The question mark, or 'interrogation point', which actually sounds rather sinister, indicates an interrogative phrase and replaces the full point at the end of the sentence in most European languages. A notable exception is Spanish, where an additional inverted question mark is also placed at the beginning of the phrase.

The Latin word *quaestiō*, meaning 'question', has been suggested as the origin of the glyph we use today as it was commonly abbreviated as a 'q' written above an 'o'.

QUOTES

Quotation marks are sometimes referred to as '66s' and '99s', indicating their form when opening and closing the quotation or phrase they attach themselves to. Dating from around the fifteenth century, quotes are used primarily to indicate a passage of direct speech. In the United Kingdom single quotes are the primary standard, while in the United States the double quote is preferred. Quotes within double quotes appear as single quotes and as double quotes when they appear within single quotes.

In some languages the curly quote is replaced by a small double chevron glyph, called a guillemet or angle quote, which sits mid-character above the baseline.

PRIMES

Primes are the bugbear of many a designer or typographer when they're used incorrectly as a substitute for an apostrophe or quote. They're small straight marks that indicate units of measurement; a single prime is used for feet and a double prime for inches. Primes are often shaped like an inverted teardrop and can be fully vertical or sloped to the right – but they're not apostrophes. If you ever see someone pointing angrily at some signage in the street with a prime used where an apostrophe or quote should be, you'll know instantly that they're a designer with a keen eye for correct glyph usage.

PARENTHESES (BRACKETS)

Parentheses, or plain old brackets, are used to pick out subordinate phrases or self contained passages within text. To be completely accurate, parentheses are round brackets. The curly or square form of brackets are named as such, and technically should not be referred to as parentheses. If you need to include brackets inside a pair of parentheses, use the square variety. Curly brackets are also known as 'braces', and angled brackets which point outwards from the contained word or phrase like arrowheads are 'chevrons'.

PILCROW

The pilcrow is also known as the paragraph mark and marks the start of a new paragraph within one long passage of text. Although fairly uncommon in everyday typesetting, the pilcrow is still used quite extensively in legal and academic writing to indicate specific paragraphs or references, and proofreaders use it to indicate the position of a fresh paragraph break. However, you'll see it every day if you use software with 'invisibles' switched on, as the pilcrow is the on-screen mark that indicates a full paragraph break.

HYPHEN

Not to be confused with em and en
dashes, a hyphen is used primarily
to join two or more words to form
a single phrase, or to separate syllables
in a word which breaks at the end
of a line of text. This technique, used
primarily but not exclusively with
justified text, is called hyphenation.

There are several types of hyphen;
they can be hard hyphens, which
always appear within the text, or soft
(optional) hyphens, which can be keyed
manually or inserted automatically by
software. Non-breaking hyphens can
also be used to keep words together
on the same line of text.

» Dash – see below
» Justified – see page 66

DASH

Dashes should not be confused with
hyphens, which are discussed above.
They're longer and appear in two main
forms, **em** dashes and **en** dashes.
An em equals the currently selected
point size in width, while an en is half
that width. The en dash usually
appears with a space on either side,
while the em dash does not. They exist
to indicate an abrupt change of
direction or thought in a sentence,
an interruption, or a span where they
effectively replace the word 'to'.
The em dash can also be used
as an alternative to a colon (:).

An em dash

» Em – see page 75
» En – see page 75

ELLIPSIS

The term ellipsis is derived from the
Ancient Greek word  *élleipsis*, which
translates as 'omission'. The glyph
consists of three full points which are
usually spaced to fill the same
character width as an **em** dash.
Typographically an ellipsis indicates
the intentional omission of text
(anything from a single word to a
longer passage) or an unfinished
thought where a sentence is left to
trail off. It can also be used to indicate
the merging of adjacent paragraphs or
statements where the second
continues the theme of the first.

» EM – SEE PAGE 75

DEGREE

The degree symbol, which dates from
the mid-sixteenth century, has several
functions; it can represent degrees of
arc in geometry or in navigational
coordinates, temperature or alcohol
proof. The glyph always appears as a
small superscript circle raised above the
baseline to align with either the cap
height or ascender line. Typographically
there should be no space between the
numeral and the glyph when it
represents degrees of arc, but a space
should be inserted after the numeral
when it represents temperature.

GLYPH (SORT)

Glyphs are subtly different to characters. A **character** is a mark that represents a specific sound (called a phoneme) or a symbol with a specific function. This means a character can be referred to generically as a glyph. A glyph, which in older movable type terminology was called a sort, can be any individual form created by a typeface designer and included in a font. For example, 'g', 'G' and '*g*' are all glyphs of the character 'g'. It can also be a combination of characters, for example a **ligature**.

» CHARACTER – SEE PAGE 52
» LIGATURE – SEE PAGE 43

DINGBAT

A dingbat is the term used to describe a printer's ornament – an additional decorative glyph included alongside the standard alphanumeric characters of a font. Dingbats were designed to fulfill various functions, including the creation of frames around headlines or page borders, and are often used as decorative bullets when a simple dot will not suffice.

There are hundreds of dingbat fonts available that cover every imaginable application but the best known has to be ITC Zapf Dingbats, thanks to its inclusion with most desktop operating systems. Dingbat fonts are often referred to as Pi fonts.

LIGATURE

A ligature is formed when two or more characters are joined to form a single glyph in order to fix the spacing issue created by the clash of adjacent characters. In the latin alphabet standard ligatures are generally limited to combinations of the lowercase characters 'i', 'f', 'h', 'j' and 'l'; examples are 'ff', 'fh', 'ffi', 'ffl', 'fi' and less commonly 'ffj'. 'Th' also crops up fairly often, particularly in Old Style and Transitional serifs.

There are several other glyphs which can be construed as ligatures but are more accurately lexical rather than typographic ligatures. For example, the glyph 'æ' is a diphthong or a double vowel sound.

INTERROBANG

This unusual glyph was invented in 1962 by a New York advertising executive named Martin K. Speckter and is named using a combination of the Latin *interrogatio*, which translates as 'rhetorical question', and the word 'bang', which is printers' slang for an exclamation point. Its first appearance in a commercial typeface came in 1966 with Richard Isbell's Americana.

Popular throughout the late 1960s and 1970s, the glyph eventually fell out of fashion, but is making something of a comeback through its inclusion in many new or updated **OpenType** glyph sets.

» OpenType – see page 76

AMPERSAND

The ampersand is a single glyph representing the word 'and'. The word ampersand is a corruption of the phrase 'and (&) per se and', which translates roughly as 'and (&) by itself is and'. Traditionally, when recited aloud, the alphabet would be completed with the phrase 'X, Y, Z and per se and…' – over the years the quickly spoken phrase morphed into a single word.

Its form originates from the ligature of the characters 'e' and 't' where *et* is latin for 'and'. Its basic form provides type designers with endless opportunity for decorative experimentation, particularly with the italic styles of serif faces.

OCTOTHORPE

Not to be confused with the musical notation for 'sharp', which leans backwards, the octothorpe is known commonly as the 'number sign' or, thanks to Twitter, 'hashtag'. American English readers will be very familiar with the octothorpe when used to abbreviate the word 'number', for example 'item #24'. European readers will recognise it but are more likely to use the abbreviation 'Nº'.

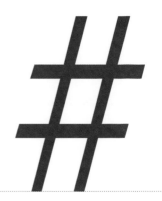

It was also known historically as the 'pound sign' and was used to represent the unit of weight (said to be a shorthand combination of 'lb' and '=') but this application is rarely if ever used today, at least in typographic terms.

@ SYMBOL

The 'at' sign began life as a shorthand accounting symbol meaning 'at a rate of' or 'each at', for example 12 cartons @ £3.80 = £45.60. For obvious reasons it was important for merchants to indicate clearly that prices were per individual item, and it's thought to have originally formed from a lowercase 'a' written inside a lowercase 'e'.

The @ has gained a new lease of life today as the vital component of all email addresses. Curiously the design of the @ can be rather unsatisfying in the case of some faces, so consider substituting another (of a compatible form) if the @ of your chosen font doesn't look the part.

COPYRIGHT

The copyright symbol that we're familiar with today was officially introduced in the United States in 1954 and subsequently adopted internationally, although proposals for the use of the © symbol were put forward as early as 1906. Prior to that the word 'copyright' or the abbreviation 'copr.' was used.

The symbol incorrectly appears as a small glyph raised above the baseline (superscript) in some typefaces, but to be typographically correct it should be a full-size glyph that sits on the baseline.

ASTERISK

As is the case with many glyphs, the asterisk derives its name from Latin and is a corruption of *asteriscus*, which translates as 'small star'. In typographic terms it's used to indicate the inclusion of a footnote, and multiple asterisks (i.e. ** or ***) may be used if more than one footnote appears. Asterisks commonly have either five or six points; traditionally, serif faces included a six-pointed asterisk, while sans serif asterisks had five, but in practice this is no longer an observed convention.

BULLET

Bullets, or in common speech bullet points, are frequently used to indicate separate items in a list that don't require a specific numbered order. It's thought that the name is derived from the shape of standard projectile bullets as, until relatively recently, bullets were cast as simple spheres or balls.

Bullets are most often circular but this isn't an unequivocal requirement; they can be square, diamond shaped or a specific glyph such as an arrowhead or a star depending on the nature of the list.

DAGGER (OBELISK)

The dagger symbol, which may also be referred to as an obelisk, performs a function broadly similar to the asterisk. However, its potential advantage is drawn from having a 'double dagger' option, as shown to the right. This means that more than one footnote can be clearly marked for any one page using the extra glyph. Daggers can also be used in conjunction with asterisks if multiple footnotes are required. Consider using a heavier weight for the dagger glyph within running text if it doesn't stand out prominently enough.

The name and origin of the glyph are thought to be Ancient Greek, where *obelos* translates as 'roasting spit'.

MANICULE

These days the manicule is most often used to create a retro design flavour, but its origins are as a mark made in the margin of a manuscript indicating a note or a correction. They date as far back as the twelfth century and are now used primarily as an elaborate attention-grabbing bullet device.

Contemporary digital typefaces have on the whole lacked a manicule glyph, leaving designers with the option of choosing a pi font such as Zapf Dingbats, but they're making a comeback in many new releases of faces with extended OpenType character sets.

Chapter 3

Type Terms

TYPEFACE

The term typeface represents the collected weights and styles of a set of fonts, independent of a specific point size, which share common visual characteristics. That would mean **Neue Swift** is an example of a typeface rather than a **font**. However, the arrival of the OpenType format has blurred this accepted definition slightly because it moves the terms Typeface and Font closer together; a single digital file now contains the information for *all* point sizes of a specific weight or style. That said, it's still helpful to think of a typeface as a collection of fonts which share specific design characteristics.

» Neue Swift – see page 126
» Font – see below

Light

Regular

Book

Semibold

Bold

FONT (FOUNT)

A font (or fount) used to be defined as all the glyphs of a specific weight or style of a typeface in a *specific* size; 10 point **Times New Roman** Regular is an example of a font. This harks back to the days of metal foundry type, where each font was a collection of individual sorts of the exact same point size. The arrival of the OpenType format for fonts has blurred this definition slightly because a single digital file now contains *all* the information for point sizes of a specific weight or style. Even so, it's still helpful to think of a font as a single specific weight or style of a typeface family.

» Times New Roman – see page 122

12 pt

24 pt

48 pt

72 pt

96 pt

WEIGHT

The words Weight and Style are interchanged loosely by designers and typographers alike, but there's a standard used throughout this book which dictates that roman fonts are referred to as weights (e.g. **Gill Sans** Book or Gill Sans Bold) while italics are referred to as accompanying styles (e.g. Gill Sans Book Italic or Gill Sans Bold Italic). The weight of a font is indicated by its stroke widths. There are, of course, also width variants, but I still tend to stick to the same convention, where **Futura** Condensed Bold would be a weight while Futura Condensed Bold Oblique is a style.

» Gill Sans – see page 154
» Futura – see page 152

Gill Sans Light

Gill Sans Book

Gill Sans Medium

Gill Sans Bold

Gill Sans Heavy

STYLE

Style is a word that can be used quite loosely to refer to any given font or variant in a typeface family; in other words any one single font. However, throughout this book italics are referred to as styles (e.g. **Bembo** Regular Italic or Bembo Bold Italic) while roman fonts are referred to as weights (e.g. Bembo Regular or Bembo Bold). There are also width variants, but the same convention, where **Univers** 57 Condensed would be a weight while Univers 57 Condensed Oblique is a style, is used throughout the book.

» Bembo – see page 102
» Univers – see page 160

Bembo Italic

Bembo Semibold Italic

Bembo Bold Italic

Bembo Extra Bold Italic

ALPHABET

The **characters** contained within a set of glyphs in any one typeface which represent specific sounds (called phonemes), so typographically the characters A–Z in either uppercase or lowercase. Other characters representing symbols or punctuation are sometimes erroneously considered to be part of the alphabet.

» CHARACTER – SEE BELOW

ABCDEFGHI
JKLMNOPQR
STUVWXYZ
abcdefghijklmn
opqrstuvwxyz

52

CHARACTER

In everyday terms a character may also be a glyph, but in typographic terms a character is a phoneme (a glyph which has a specific sound) or a symbol with a specific function. For example, a lowercase 'b' is a character, but it can be set as a roman 'b', an italic '*b*' or even a small cap 'ʙ', all of which are individual glyphs with their own unique Unicode encoding. Unicode is the international computing industry standard for the handling of text and currently encompasses more than 120,000 individual characters. When talking type, it's important to understand the subtle difference between a character and a glyph.

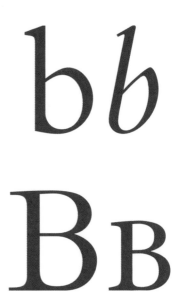

METRICS

The term metrics, when applied to typography and typefaces, refers in general to the various vertical and horizontal proportions of the letterforms. For example, there are five accepted vertical measurements (or metrics) in type design; ascender line, cap height, the midline, baseline and descender line. However, there are also overshoots where round characters or the odd vertex descend below the baseline. One can also talk about the junction height for characters such as the 'B', 'P' and 'R', and about the lowercase 't' height, which is usually different to any other character. All these (and more) can be referred to collectively as the metrics of a typeface.

Ascender line, cap height, midline, baseline and descender line

SIDEBEARING

A font's letterspacing properties are governed by two things; the left and right sidebearings. The idea of sidebearings has remained relatively unchanged since the days of metal type, when each character sat within a **body** at the end of a metal sort. As the sorts were set side-by-side, the sidebearings (or the distances between the characters and the edges of each block) governed the letterspacing. Today, sidebearings are of course virtual and a lot easier to tune if letterspacing needs to be adjusted, but the principles behind them are the same. The data controlling the width of sidebearings is embedded in all digital fonts.

» Body – see page 32

UPPERCASE (MAJUSCULE)

The large characters that make up an alphabet. The term uppercase, like many typographic terms, is derived from the days of hand-set metal foundry type. The individual glyphs, or sorts, were stored in special trays with consistently placed ompartments for each glyph. Compositors would then know exactly where to reach for an 'A' or a 'K', speeding up the otherwise laborious process. These trays were stored in racks with the uppercase tray placed above the **lowercase** tray, thus providing us with the term uppercase.

» Lowercase – see below

ABCDEFG
HIJKLMN
OPQRSTU
VWXYZ

LOWERCASE (MINUSCULE)

The small characters that make up an alphabet. The term lowercase, like many typographic terms, is derived from the days of hand-set metal foundry type. The individual glyphs, or sorts, were stored in special trays with consistently placed compartments for each glyph. This meant a compositor would know exactly where to reach for an 'e' or an 'x', speeding up the otherwise laborious process. These trays were stored in racks with the lowercase tray placed below the **uppercase** tray, thus providing us with the term lowercase.

» Uppercase – see above

abcdefg
hijklmn
opqrstu
vwxyz

BICAMERAL

An alphabet which contains both uppercase and lowercase characters is bicameral. Bicameral character sets are normal for most Latin alphabets, particularly those designed for text setting, but there are plenty of display faces in existence that only contain uppercase characters, making them **unicameral**.

» Unicameral – see below

AaBbCcDdEe
FfGgHhIiJjKk
LlMmNnOoPp
QqRrSsTtUu
VvWwXxYyZz

UNICAMERAL

An alphabet which contains *only* uppercase *or* lowercase characters is unicameral. Unicameral character sets are not the norm in Latin alphabets designed for text setting, but there are plenty of unicameral display faces in existence. An alphabet with both uppercase and lowercase characters is termed **bicameral**.

The example shown to the right is a revival of Universal, an experimental face designed at the Bauhaus by Herbert Bayer in the late 1920s. A display face such **Perpetua** Titling provides us with a further example.

» Bicameral – see above
» Perpetua – see page 118

abcdef
ghijklm
nopqrst
uvwxyz

ROMAN

In typographic terms roman can (somewhat confusingly) mean two things, but when used in context both meanings make sense. Firstly it can mean the standard or upright style of a typeface, and secondly it can be used to denote the regular weight of a typeface. For example, one could say that a typeface family contains only roman weights with no accompanying italic styles, or that the regular weight of Bodoni is named 'Bodoni Roman' rather than 'Bodoni Italic'.

Take care to always use a lowercase 'r' for the term unless it begins a sentence or is incorporated into a font's name. When used in a sentence, Roman with an uppercase 'R' means a person from Rome.

rome

ITALIC

Italics first appeared in Italy at the very beginning of the sixteenth century; the printer Aldus Manutius and the punchcutter Francesco Griffo are credited with the creation of the first movable italic type. There are two distinct styles of italic. Cursive italics (or true italics) resemble handwritten letterforms, and characteristically always feature a **single-storey** 'a'. **Oblique roman** italics lack the cursive forms and are sloped versions of the roman characters. There are a handful of typefaces, **Joanna** being one of them, that mix oblique romans with a few cursive letterforms.

Cursive   Oblique roman

» Single-storey – see page 61
» Oblique roman – see page 57
» Joanna – see page 120

OBLIQUE ROMAN

Oblique romans lack the cursive form associated with many Humanist, Old Style or Transitional serif typefaces. Instead, an oblique roman takes the form of a sloped version of the standard roman weights, but there's more to it than simply adding a slant. When a glyph is sloped to the right, distortion occurs in curved elements of a letterform, so type designers make small optical adjustments to strokes in order to correct any visual anomalies. This is the reason why creating *faux* oblique romans by adding a slope to a roman weight is a typographic no-no. If a typeface doesn't contain true **italic** or oblique roman styles and you need to use them, choose another typeface.

» Italic – see page 56

BACK SLANT

If a typeface includes italic styles they generally slope to the right as either a cursive or an oblique roman form. However, a relative minority of typefaces contain styles of italic that slope to the left. This left-leaning slope is referred to as a back slant. Using a back slant with left-to-right-reading copy isn't recommended as it opposes the natural flow of the text.

SLOPE

Slope refers to the angle at which a typeface's cursive **italic** or **oblique roman** glyphs are inclined. Slope is usually biased to the right but can also lean to the left, although this is relatively rare as left-leaning faces don't follow the natural flow of Western-style left-right reading. It's not recommended that a slope value be added to a roman font to create a *faux* italic as this produces distorted letterforms that don't replicate a properly drawn oblique roman. Slope shouldn't be confused with **axis**, which is the invisible line that indicates the angle of stress of a typeface or font.

» Italic – see page 56
» Oblique roman – see page 57
» Axis – see page 24

OPTICAL SIZES

In the days of hand cut metal type, a skilled punchcutter would make subtle adjustments to stroke widths and proportions for each point size to maintain visual consistency. Text faces must be clear and open (yet robust) to maintain legibility, but use them at 72 point and letterforms may look too bold or even overly crude. Many typeface families now contain text, caption, subhead and display weights intended for use at specific size ranges, and these are termed optical sizes. Text fonts will commonly feature thicker strokes or more robust serifs, while at the other end of the scale the display weights will be altogether finer in construction.

Text

Caption

Subhead

Display

CONTRAST

The difference in thickness between the thickest and thinnest parts of a glyph's stroke. One of the principal indicators of a typeface's classification, contrast varies considerably from typeface to typeface but is generally the same (or at least very similar) from one glyph to another in any one font.
To give an example, the Rational Serif **Bodoni** is a high contrast typeface, while the Geometric Sans Serif **Futura** has practically no contrast at all in its strokes. The distinctive contrast associated with each category of type classification is explained in more detail in chapter four of this book.

» BODONI – SEE PAGE 110
» FUTURA – SEE PAGE 152

HAIRLINE

A hairline is the thinnest part of a letterform *excepting* a serif. The best example of a hairline would be something like the crossbar of the 'H' in a Rational Serif such as **Bodoni**, where the serifs are equally as thin as the hairline. The greater degree of contrast that's displayed by a typeface, the more obvious the hairlines are.

» BODONI – SEE PAGE 110

BOLDFACE

Technically, the term boldface can be applied to any bold font that constitutes part of a typeface family, but in its modern incarnation it tends to be used more often to describe any overtly heavy display typeface designed to draw attention by way of a headline or banner.

Always select the correct bold weights of a typeface from your type menu rather than a *faux* bold created with a click of a control bar button. The latter will likely produce a distorted character shape that is neither roman nor bold, but something in between the two.

NOVELTY TYPE

Professional designers and typographers have a tendency to shun novelty typefaces, but they do have their uses and deserve to be given serious consideration, as many of them are actually cleverly conceived and well constructed. A novelty typeface can be anything that's overtly decorative and doesn't fit neatly into any other typeface classification. Novelty faces are meant almost exclusively for display use. When used in an appropriate way, and combined with other more 'serious' fonts, novelty (or ornamental) faces can inject a sense of fun or historical identity that would otherwise be difficult to achieve.

SINGLE-STOREY

The term describing any lowercase 'a' which has a single bowl without a finial arm above it. It can also describe a lowercase 'g' which has a single bowl with a stem and a tail below it. The typeface **Futura** features a single-storey 'a' and 'g'.

A single-storey 'a' is generally thought to have a lower level of readability than a **double-storey** 'a' because of its visual similarity to the lowercase 'o'.

» FUTURA – SEE PAGE 152
» DOUBLE-STOREY – SEE BELOW

DOUBLE-STOREY

The term for any lowercase 'a' which has a bowl with a stem and a finial arm above it. It can also describe a lowercase 'g' which has a bowl with an ear, and a linked loop below it. This style of 'g' can also be referred to as 'binocular'. The typeface **Baskerville** features a double-storey 'a' and 'g'.

A double-storey 'a' is generally thought to have a greater level of readability than a **single-storey** 'a', as it looks less like an 'o'.

» BASKERVILLE – SEE PAGE 108
» SINGLE-STOREY – SEE ABOVE

CALLIGRAPHIC

Calligraphy is the art of hand lettering with either a pen or a brush, so in typographic terms 'calligraphic' can be applied to any typeface that has Humanist qualities, meaning the glyphs have some appearance of being written or drawn by hand. The word calligraphy originates from the Greek word *kalligraphia*, which roughly translates as 'beautiful writing'. Take care when choosing overtly calligraphic typefaces, and always consider whether a good cursive italic might be more appropriate for your subject matter.

SWASH CHARACTER

A swash is created by modifying or embellishing an existing component of a glyph. Swashes can take the form of exaggerated serifs, extended tails or terminals or embellished strokes, and date back to the early sixteenth century. It was around this time that **italics** first appeared. Italics and swashes can both be linked to the style of handwriting from that period. Swashes are generally linked to serif typefaces, and more often to italic styles. If a face is supplied with swash characters, they can be applied automatically using the advanced features of **OpenType**.

» ITALIC – SEE PAGE 56
» OPENTYPE – SEE PAGE 76

INLINE FONT

Most people would know that
an outline font has a thin rule (or
keyline) that faithfully follows the
outline shape of the standard
characters, leaving the main stems
and strokes contained within as
empty space. Inline fonts are different
because the keylines that define their
outlines are often thicker, leaving a
narrow 'inline' at the centre of strokes
and stems. Inline fonts can also
feature open ended strokes.

The example shown to the right is
from the newly released Gill Sans
Nova family. The display face
Industria Inline from Linotype
provides us with another example.

CHROMATIC TYPE

Chromatic fonts such as **Lulo** shown
to the right are layered typeface
families that can be combined to
create characters with more than one
colour or texture. In use, text is input
using one of the regular fonts in the
package, the text box or container
is then duplicated to align both
horizontally and vertically with the
original, and an alternative font style
such as an outline or drop shadow is
applied. In this way, fully editable
characters of more than one colour can
be built. Clearly these faces are best
suited for display, and have become
increasingly popular in recent years.

» Lulo – see page 184

CONDENSED

A term reserved for typefaces or weights within a larger typeface family that are narrower than the regular weights and styles, making them useful for setting text that has to fit within a narrow measure. Condensed faces can also be useful for captions, footnotes and annotation when space is at a premium. A good condensed face should retain the legibility of its regular width siblings in the typeface family if it's to be suitable for setting text at smaller point sizes.

Many typeface families, for example Akzidenz-Grotesk, Franklin Gothic, Frutiger and Univers, contain condensed weights.

COMPRESSED

A term reserved for typefaces or weights within a larger typeface family that have narrower widths than both their regular and condensed counterparts. They also characteristically tend to appear a little darker than condensed typefaces. This means compressed (or ultra condensed) faces are generally, but not exclusively, better suited for display use as they can be less legible at smaller point sizes.

Many typeface families, for example Benton Sans, Helvetica and Franklin Gothic, contain compressed weights.

EXPANDED (EXTENDED)

A term reserved for typefaces or weights within a larger typeface family that have distinctly wider character widths than their regular width counterparts. Most importantly, no extra weight or thickness is added to the stems or strokes of expanded characters or glyphs.

Many typeface families, for example Century, Helvetica and Univers, contain expanded weights.

COLOUR

Typographic colour denotes the tonal value or overall darkness of a complete block of running text, expressed as a greyscale value. As well as the design of the letterforms of a font, point size, letterspacing and leading can influence colour.

Don't confuse colour with weight; a bolder font will clearly create a darker colour on the page than its lighter sibling as there is more ink and less paper; typographic colour should be judged more by the merits of different typefaces in comparison with one another. To gauge typographic colour, try squinting at the page so the text blurs slightly.

Lorem ipsum dolor sit amet, consectetuer adipiscing elit, sed diam nonummy nibh euismod tincidunt ut laoreet dolore magna aliquam erat volutpat. Ut wisi enim ad minim veniam, quis nostrud exerci tation ullamcorper suscipit lobortis nisl ut aliquip ex ea commodo consequat. Duis autem vel eum iriure dolor in hendrerit in vulputate velit esse molestie consequat, vel illum

8/11 pt Baskerville Regular

Lorem ipsum dolor sit amet, consectetuer adipiscing elit, sed diam nonummy nibh euismod tincidunt ut laoreet dolore magna aliquam erat volutpat. Ut wisi enim ad minim veniam, quis nostrud exerci tation ullamcorper suscipit lobortis nisl ut aliquip ex ea commodo consequat. Duis autem vel eum iriure dolor in hendrerit

8/11 pt Sabon Roman

ALIGNMENT

Text is generally set to align against an invisible axis which is vertical in most cases and can be either at the left, at the right or in the centre of the text block. Text aligning to the left is termed either flush left (where all lines of text begin at the same left-hand axis) or ragged right (where lines terminate at different points on the right side of the text block). Subsequently, text which aligns to a right-hand axis is termed flush right or ragged left. Text aligning to a central axis is termed **centred**, and free-form text which doesn't match any of the above criteria has asymmetrical alignment.

» CENTRED – SEE PAGE 67

Ranged left   Centred   Ranged right

JUSTIFIED

Justified text ranges with invisible axes at both of the outer edges of a column and is achieved by making small spacing adjustments to inter-character and inter-word spacing across a full line of text. This was a difficult task prior to digital typesetting, but now software and font data combine to make automatic adjustments when justified text is specified. However, manual intervention is sometimes required to avoid typographic hazards such as overly wide spacing between words. Justified text is particularly popular with book designers handling large volumes of continuous text, as in a novel, and works best when the **measure** is fairly wide.

» MEASURE – SEE PAGE 71

Justified

CENTRED

Blocks of running text tend to be either **flush left** or **flush right** but can also be centred, meaning the lines of text are arranged symmetrically on an invisible central axis. Centred text is useful in a raft of situations such as headlines, introductory paragraphs or one-off quotations, but be aware that it's not always the most legible choice for large amounts of running text because each line starts at a different point. Additionally, mixing centred text with ranged text is a typographic no-no, so if your text is ranged left it's usually best to avoid centred headlines and/or centred cross headings.

Centred

» Alignment – see page 66

COPYFITTING

In the pre-digital world, copyfitting was an essential skill that had to be mastered by all typographers and graphic designers. The term refers to the technique used to estimate the number of characters or words per line, thus indicating the amount of vertical space that a typed manuscript will take up when set in a particular font at a particular point size. We can, of course, now run the text directly into a layout and see exactly how much space it takes up, but a basic (and intuitive) level of copyfitting skill is still very useful when assessing how a new layout might work.

KERNING

This important term describes the technique employed when adjusting the small spaces between individual characters in a word to improve legibility, and to create typography that is visually pleasing to the eye. Software applies automatic kerning using kerning tables (data embedded into fonts), but 'automatic' doesn't always equal 'correct', and characters sometimes crunch into one another or appear too far apart, so manual kerning is a skill all designers should master. **Ligatures** exist to alleviate the problem of character pairs which are difficult to kern, for example fi or fl.

Without kerning

With kerning

» LIGATURES – SEE PAGE 43

68

TRACKING (LETTERSPACING)

Tracking refers to the letterspacing applied to a full line or paragraph of text, and shouldn't be confused with **kerning**. Entering a positive tracking value relaxes the spacing between characters, while a negative value tightens it. The application of any level of tracking should be approached with caution, particularly in the case of running text, where legibility and therefore readability can be ruined by over zealous tracking. Headlines, on the other hand, can often benefit from a little negative tracking as inter-character spacing can appear to open up at larger point sizes.

-50 tracking

Xxxxx

0 tracking

+50 tracking

Xxxxx

+100 tracking

» KERNING – SEE ABOVE

LEADING
(LINE SPACING)

Also known as line feed, leading represents the distance in points, from one baseline to the next, between successive lines of text. The term originates from the days of hand-set foundry type when lead strips were manually inserted between lines of metal type to separate them. Leading is usually set at a larger value than the point size of the type to ensure **ascenders** and **descenders** don't clash. When leading is set to the same value as that of the type's point size, the text is said to be **solid set**.

12 pt leading

18 pt leading

24 pt leading

» ASCENDERS – SEE PAGE 16
» DESCENDERS – SEE PAGE 16
» SOLID SET – SEE BELOW

SOLID SET

When **leading** is set to the same value as point size, the text is said to be 'solid set'. The term originates from the days of hand-set foundry type when lead strips were manually inserted between lines of metal type to separate them. If no lead was inserted, the sorts were 'solid set' against one another. Leading is usually set at a larger value than the point size of the type to ensure **ascenders** and **descenders** don't clash. It's now possible to set leading to a value less than that of the point size being used, so beware of extender clashes and the negative effect this might have on legibility.

Solid setting, for example 12/12 pt represented graphically here, allows very little vertical space for ascenders and descenders.

» LEADING – SEE ABOVE
» ASCENDER – SEE PAGE 16
» DESCENDER – SEE PAGE 16

ORPHAN

An orphan indicates text that is overly short, maybe one or two words, in the final line of a paragraph of text. It can also mean a single line stranded at the bottom of a column of text, separated from the rest of its paragraph at the top of the following column or the next page. This is one of the principal typographic crimes committed by non-professional typographers and designers, and should be avoided at all costs. If this occurs during the design and layout process, look for a longer line above the orphan that can be turned over, thus pushing one or two additional words over to help fill out the short line, or to create an additional line, thus removing the orphan.

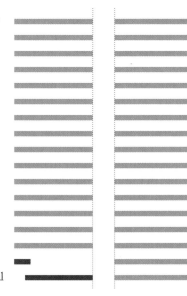

70

WIDOW

A widow is a single line falling at the end of a paragraph which finds itself stranded at the top of a column of text, separated from the rest of its paragraph at the base of the previous column or page. This is avoided by professional typographers and designers but is a mistake that is often made by non-professionals. If it occurs during the design and layout process, look for a preceding line that can be shortened, thus allowing the widow to run back.

MEASURE
(COLUMN WIDTH)

The length of a line of text expressed in a variety of units including millimetres, points or picas. This differs from **leading**, which is now almost always expressed in points as it relates closely to type size. Short measures can be problematic as they create awkward line breaks for anything other than text set at small point sizes. Research has shown that the optimal character count per line for any given measure is between 50–60 characters including spaces, but 40–70 still allows for good readability, where the eye can easily locate the start of successive lines of text.

» Leading – see page 69

GUTTER

A gutter can be defined as the white space between two columns of text on a single page, or the space between a column of text and the spine at the centre of a book or magazine. Don't confuse the term with 'margin', which defines the space at the outer edges of a page. If you're using **flush left** text, the gutter may be fairly narrow as the irregular line endings will naturally form extra white space between columns. If you're setting your text with **justified** alignment, a wider gutter may be necessary to sufficiently differentiate the space between each column.

» Flush left – see page 66
» Justified – see page 66

CICERO

A cicero is a unit of measurement unique to typography and used in continental Europe, primarily by the French and the Italians, although less so since the advent of desktop publishing. It's a very old standard and was first used in a fifteenth-century edition of Cicero's *Epistulae ad Familiares*, which provided the measure with its name. One cicero was equal to ⅙ of the historical French inch, which is in turn equal to twelve Didot points or 4.5 mm.

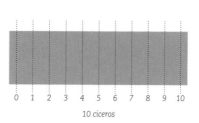
10 ciceros

The desktop publishing point, or PostScript point, has usurped many of the older typographic measurements for everyday use, so one cicero now equals 12.788 points.

PICA

A pica is a unit of measurement which originated in France in the late eighteenth century. Devised by François-Ambroise Didot, it offered an alternative to the **cicero** and under the contemporary computer point standard is equal to 12 points, or ¹⁄₇₂ of an international foot, or ⅙ of an inch, or 4.233 mm. In the US a pica is ever so slightly smaller at ¹⁄₇₂.₂₇ of a foot, or 4.2175 mm. Also, one computer pica equals 12 pixels on a computer screen.

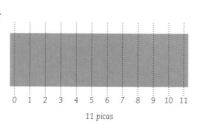
11 picas

If you use picas with a publishing application such as Adobe InDesign, measurements are represented as full picas followed by points; 7½ picas (7 picas and 6 points) would read 7p6.

» CICERO – SEE ABOVE

POINT

A point is a unit of measurement used primarily to indicate type size and **leading**. Points are also often used by designers for all vertical measurements incorporated into a typographic grid to ensure baselines align correctly with other non-typographic content.

A computer point (the standard since the advent of desktop publishing) is equal to ½ of an inch, or 0.353 mm. Point size refers to the height of the **body** of a font, not the height of the characters or glyphs. It's interesting to note that, because of this, fonts with a large x-height appear larger on the page than those with a smaller x-height when set at the same point size.

0   12   24   36   48   60   72   84   96   108 120 132

11 picas = 132 points

x   X   X   X

12 pt   *24 pt*   *48 pt*   *72 pt*

» LEADING – SEE PAGE 69
» BODY – SEE PAGE 32

HARD SPACE (NON-BREAKING)

The term non-breaking space is in some ways more appropriate than hard space because it's worded as such in the Adobe InDesign menu, but hard space is the traditional typographic term for a space between words that will not break at the end of a line of text. There are two types of hard space – fixed and flexible. If you use flexible spaces, words will space themselves evenly across a measure when set as **justified** text. If you use fixed spaces, the non-breaking words will bunch together, as illustrated to the right, leaving larger gaps between groups of words.

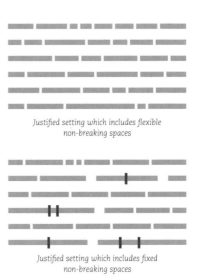

Justified setting which includes flexible non-breaking spaces

Justified setting which includes fixed non-breaking spaces

» JUSTIFIED – SEE PAGE 66

THICK SPACE

A thick space is a measure equal to ⅓ of an em in width, where a full em is equal to the currently selected point size of the type. If you're an Adobe InDesign user, there is no menu option for a thick space but there is an option for a 'Third Space', which corresponds to a traditional thick space. When should one use a thick space? Well, it's slightly wider than a standard character space (the clue is in the term's name), so if you'd like to create slightly wider word spacing whilst having more control over the size of that space, the thick space is an appropriate choice.

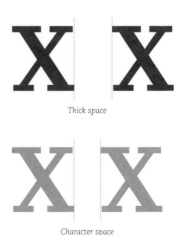

Thick space

Character space

THIN SPACE

A thin space is a measure equal to ⅕ of an em in width, where a full em is equal to the currently selected point size of the type. If you're an Adobe InDesign user, there's a dedicated menu option allowing you to insert a thin space as required. When should one use a thin space? Well, it's slightly narower than a standard character space (the clue is in the term's name), so if you'd like to close up your word spacing whilst having more control over the value of the spacing, the thin space is an appropriate choice.

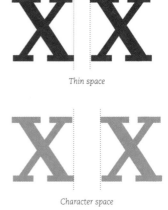

Thin space

Character space

EM

A unit of measurement equal to a font's point size; for example, if you are using 12-point type an em will measure 12 points. In the days of metal type an em was defined by the width of a font's widest glyph, which is almost always the uppercase 'M', hence the name for this term. Today it's rare for an 'M' to match the width of an em precisely.

Generally, an em also equals the length of a font's em **dash** or em space but there are exceptions with some typefaces. Traditionally, printers referred to an em as a 'mutton'.

» DASH – SEE PAGE 40

EN

A unit of measurement equal to half the width of an **em**, or half the current point size; if you are using 12-point type an en will measure 6 points.

Generally, an en also equals the length of a font's en dash or en space but there are exceptions with some typefaces. Traditionally printers referred to an en as a 'nut'.

» EM – SEE ABOVE

POSTSCRIPT

The desktop publishing revolution was built around PostScript, the outline font format developed by Adobe and introduced in 1984. PostScript fonts consist of two separate files – a printer font which contains the outline information for each glyph, and a screen font which renders the text on a display. Although the superior **OpenType** format has replaced PostScript as the format of choice for today's font designers, there are still thousands of PostScript fonts in regular use, and the original Type 1 format is still fully supported by the majority of major operating systems and design applications.

» OPENTYPE – SEE BELOW

Printer font

Screen font

OPENTYPE

OpenType is a flexible and relatively new font format developed jointly by Adobe and Microsoft. It's a cross platform format which works on both Macs and PCs, and can contain up to 65,536 separate glyphs in a single font file, making the need for **expert sets** a thing of the past. If that isn't enough, software such as Adobe's InDesign can take advantage of built-in features such as contextual glyph substitution, discretionary ligatures, swash characters and so on. The advent of OpenType has heralded an explosion in the creation of formal and casual script typefaces which have benefited enormously from the advanced features offered by the OpenType format.

» EXPERT SET – SEE PAGE 77

EXPERT SET

Before the advent of **OpenType**, **PostScript** Type 1 font files could only contain a maximum of 256 separate glyphs, limiting the number of alternative glyphs that could be included. To alleviate the problem, selected high quality fonts were supplied with 'expert sets' containing, for example, small caps, oldstyle numerals, additional ligatures, extra fractions and so on.

The expanded capabilities of OpenType have rendered expert sets obsolete for newly released typefaces but many designers still actively use the older PostScript format.

» OPENTYPE – SEE PAGE 76
» POSTSCRIPT – SEE PAGE 76

ABCD

1328

$\frac{2}{3}$ $\frac{3}{8}$ $\frac{7}{8}$

SMALL CAPS

Small caps were included in the **expert sets** of PostScript fonts but are now included in single OpenType font files, and can be accessed via the advanced functionality of the format. Small caps are approximately, but not exclusively, the same height as lowercase characters, but are not simply 'shrunken' uppercase glyphs. Type designers will invariably make subtle adjustments to stroke weights and proportions when drawing the small cap glyphs, so avoid using *faux* small caps created by publishing software as they won't look right. Small caps are great for headings but not running text, as they lack the legibility of lowercase characters.

Nn

» EXPERT SET – SEE ABOVE

FOLIO

The term for the page number in the layout of a book or magazine. Folios can be placed anywhere on the page – there is no steadfast convention – but their position should be governed by the need for clear navigation. It's not necessary to include a folio on every single page, and convention indicates that pages that appear before a contents list often don't include folios, but if a folio is omitted from one page or spread it's a good idea to try to include one on the following page. Folios are usually numerical, but can be substituted for sequenced characters in the case of front matter, appendices and so on.

9

ix

OLDSTYLE FIGURES

Oldstyle figures vary in height with some dipping prominently below the baseline (although technically all numerals do share a common baseline) making them the opposite of **lining figures**. They blend well with running text because they're visually harmonious when set with mixed uppercase and lowercase characters. Lining figures tend to stand out more prominently in running text.
OpenType faces often include both lining and oldstyle figures, providing maximum flexibility for designers.

X136

» LINING FIGURES – SEE PAGE 79
» OPENTYPE – SEE PAGE 76

LINING FIGURES

Lining figures are the opposite of **oldstyle figures** and are roughly equal in height to the uppercase characters of a font. It's popular for lining figures to be the default setting for most fonts as they stand out more in running text, and they should always be used when set alongside uppercase text. On the other hand, if you want numerals to blend into the text, oldstyle figures with their varying heights work better. **OpenType** faces often include both lining and oldstyle figures, providing maximum flexibility for designers.

» OLDSTYLE FIGURES – SEE PAGE 78
» OPENTYPE – SEE PAGE 76

X136

TABULAR FIGURES

Lining and **oldstyle** figures are proportional, meaning they have varying body widths depending on the width of each character. Tabular figures can be either lining or oldstyle but are different because they have identical body widths, meaning they're monospaced. This is particularly useful for aligning columns of figures vertically, as in a timetable, hence the term tabular figures. Tabular lining figures tend to work best in terms of legibility, but tabular oldstyle figures work better if an historical feel is required.

» LINING FIGURES – SEE ABOVE
» OLDSTYLE FIGURES – SEE PAGE 78

623.456
456.623

Tabular lining

123.456
456.123

Proportional lining

DROP CAP

An uppercase character at the beginning of a paragraph that is set to a depth of at least two lines of the body copy. The drop cap (sometimes also referred to as an initial cap) is often set in a heavier weight of the text face, but can also be set in an entirely different typeface to create a potentially greater visual impact. Drop caps always cut into the area occupied by the body copy and never sit proud of the first line. An initial cap that shares its baseline with the first line of text is an **elevated cap**.

» Elevated cap – see below

L orem ips
amet, co
adipiscing el
nonummy ni
tincidunt ut
dolore magn

ELEVATED CAP

An uppercase character at the beginning of a paragraph that shares its baseline with the first line of text but is set at a larger point size, giving it a larger cap height than the body copy. The elevated cap (sometimes also referred to as an initial cap) is often set in a heavier weight of the text face, but can also be set in an entirely different typeface to create a potentially greater visual impact. Don't confuse elevated caps with **drop caps**, which always cut into the area occupied by the body copy.

» Drop cap – see above

Lorem ipsu
amet, consec
adipiscing eli
nonummy ni
tincidunt ut l

VERSAL

A versal is a **drop cap** or an **elevated cap** which has been ornamented in some way. Versals originated in illuminated medieval manuscripts and their use today is naturally limited to niche publications and facsimiles of historical publications. It's unlikely that you'll find a character resembling a versal in any standard character set, but there are certainly faces available that replicate the uncial letterforms of the Middle Ages and can therefore provide you with a platform on which to base your own version of a medieval versal glyph.

» Drop cap – see page 80
» Elevated cap – see page 80

Lorem ipsu
amet, consec
adipiscing eli
nonummy ni
tincidunt ut l

BLOCK QUOTE

A block quote, which can also be referred to as a long quotation or an extract, is a quotation set concurrently with other running text and distinguished by an indent, an alternative typeface or font style or some other typographic device. To qualify as a block quote, it's generally recommended that the highlighted text should be at least one hundred words or more long. Block quotes should not be confused with pull quotes, which are shorter repeated excerpts that are not set within the run of the text and do not have to be a verbatim copy of the original text.

FOUNDRY

The word foundry means any factory that produces metal castings. In the case of type foundries, the term has stuck ever since the days of metal foundry type, where foundries linked to the type industry manufactured sorts (individual glyphs) for hand-set foundry type, and matrices for casting type for the Monotype and Linotype mechanical typesetting machines. By the late 1950s, when usable phototypesetting machines first appeared, foundries began producing 'cold type' for use with the new technology, and by the late 1980s and early 1990s the first digital foundries to *never* produce a single weight of 'physical' type had opened their doors.

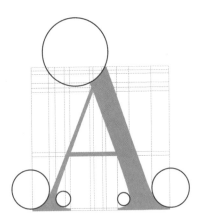

MATRIX

In typographic terms a matrix is a mould employed to cast each individual glyph for use with either the Linotype or Monotype hot metal typesetting machines. The Linotype used individual matrices stored in a pre-loaded magazine that dropped down to form a slug (or a line-o-type), which was cast in one piece and assembled as stacked rows of type. The Monotype system used a matrix case containing all of a font's glyphs, and cast individual sorts which were assembled as rows of type by the casting machine. The Linotype system was quicker, but the Monotype system, with its separate sorts, was easier to correct by hand using spare foundry type of the same font.

l	t	!	'	'	.	,	i		l	[	i	l	.	,	'	'
I	j	ſ	i	(	]	/	j		f	-	:	;	)	**f**	**t**	j
?	:	;	z	c	r	s	e	t	s	r	**s**	**r**	-	**I**	**:**	**;**
z	J	s	q	g	v	b	o	c	z	I	?	**e**	**c**	**z**	**?**	
P	*I*	y	a	-	3	6	9		a	g	**b**	**J**	v	9	6	3
C	F	x	h	£	7	4	1	0	**S**	y	**d**	**q**	0	1	4	7
L	T	k	d	.	2	5	8	o	**o**	a	**p**	**g**	**x**	8	5	2
Q	B	o	*J*	*S*	*fi*	*p*	q	p	d	y	x	**u**	**n**	**h**	**k**	**C**
V	G	R	E	A	*n*	*u*	n	u	b	v	k	h	fi	fl	S	J
K	Y	X	H	N	D	U	*ff*	*C*	*Q*	C	Z	ff	**T**	**L**	**P**	**F**
M	*G*	*O*	F	P	L	T	*w*	**E**	**N**	**Q**	**O**	**B**	**G**	**V**	**Y**	**Z**
Z	*L*	*E*	V	G	B	O	E	Q	A	w	**w**	**A**	**D**	**R**	**U**	**X**
w	*V*	*F*	*B*	*R*	*P*	*A*	*T*	*m*	D	N	R	U	Y	&	**H**	**K**
X	*K*	*Y*	*U*	*H*	*N*	*D*	ffl	ffi	m	M	H	K	X	**m**	**M**	**ffi**
Æ	*Æ*	+	*W*	*Œ*	*M*	*&*	W	Œ	**W**	...	&	—	..	%		

The position of the glyphs in a typical Monotype matrix case. The layout allows for setting in roman and bold weights, roman italics and roman small caps.

METAL TYPE (FOUNDRY TYPE)

The collective term for any characters or glyphs cast in metal and used for letterpress printing. As a subset of this, the term foundry type applies to characters or glyphs cast at the end of individual metal sticks called sorts which pre-date the mechanical typesetting machines made by Monotype and Linotype. Sorts were used for hand composed typesetting and were stored in special **uppercase** and **lowercase** trays.

» UPPERCASE – SEE PAGE 54
» LOWERCASE – SEE PAGE 54

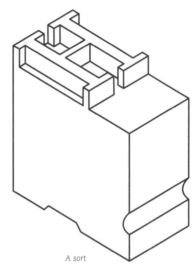

A sort

FLEURON

A fleuron is a **dingbat** which takes on the appearance of a leaf or flower. This antiquated printer's term is derived from the Old French word *floron*, meaning flower. Fleurons were also referred to traditionally as 'printer's flowers'.

Aside from dedicated dingbat fonts such as Botanical or Decoration Pi, fleurons tend to appear in historical serif typefaces such as Jenson, Caslon or Garamond.

» DINGBAT – SEE PAGE 42

BITMAP

A bitmap font is formed from pixels (square dots) and can also be referred to as a 'screen font' when bitmaps work in tandem with outline fonts (or printer fonts); the bitmaps render the font on screen and the outlines render the font when output to a printer. Outline fonts are fully scalable as they are formed from mathematical (Bézier) curves. Bitmaps, on the other hand, are resolution dependent, with resolution representing the number of pixels per inch. Older **PostScript** fonts comprise two files, a bitmap and an outline, but the more advanced **OpenType** format eschews this and consists of just one scalable font file.

» PostScript – see page 76
» OpenType – see page 76

ANTI-ALIASING

The technique known as anti-aliasing is employed to 'smooth' the edges of characters or glyphs on screen using subtle gradations of intermediate tint or tone, thus optimizing the definition of the glyph shapes we see. Today, screen resolutions are much higher than they were twenty-five years ago, but the fonts we view on those screens are still composed of pixels and are therefore still subject to rasterization, where individual pixels are visible at the edges of a digital image, particularly in curved sections. Anti-aliasing creates the impression that the type is rendered at a higher resolution, and is further improved by **hinting**.

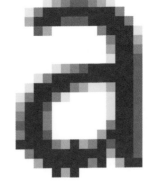

» Hinting – see page 85

HINTING

Hinting (also known as instructing) is the technique used by type designers to ensure type is rendered more accurately when displayed on screen. Mathematical instructions, which can be applied automatically by software or manually by the type designer, are embedded in the font file and are critical for producing legible text which closely resembles the actual outlines of a font's characters. It requires a large amount of skill on the part of the type designer to manually hint type. Hinting improves on the basic level of automatic **anti-aliasing**.

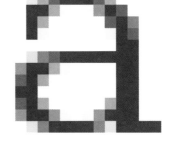

» ANTI-ALIASING – SEE PAGE 84

FAMILY

In typographic terms, a family represents the collective weights and accompanying styles of all the fonts that make up a complete typeface. In the earliest days of mechanical typesetting a family may have consisted of just two weights plus two styles; a roman with an italic style and a bold with a bold italic style. Nowadays, typeface families are typically much larger; for example, Monotype's recent update of Gill Sans, Gill Sans Nova, contains a whopping forty-three separate fonts.

Roman

Italic

Bold

Bold Italic

Chapter 4

Type Classification

ANCIENT (PRE-VENETIAN)

Ancient isn't really a *true* type classification as it covers the style of handwritten letterforms created prior to the mid-fifteenth century and the invention of movable type. The letterforms cut and cast for Johannes Gutenberg's famous *42-line Bible* were based very closely on the accepted style of handwriting used in Germany at the time and, although essentially a Blackletter, it helps to broadly represent this 'pre-typeface' group.

ALOT Gutenberg

BLACKLETTER (TEXTURA, FRAKTUR)

Blackletter typefaces first appeared in the mid-fifteenth century and can be sub-divided into several categories, the main two being Texturas and Frakturs. Texturas generally feature straight strokes (with few curves) and additional finely detailed decorative strokes with sharp finials. Fraktur faces (which appeared later) feature both straight and curved strokes; the lowercase 'o' is a useful character to check when distinguishing one Blackletter category from another.

Wilhelm Klingspor Schrift

HUMANIST SERIF (VENETIAN)

The original 'roman' typefaces that we're used to reading today, Humanist Serifs appeared in the later years of the fifteenth century. Letterforms are distinctly calligraphic; they appear to have been written with a broad-nibbed pen held at a constant angle to the paper. Stroke contrast is generally low to moderate, x-heights are relatively low and the terminals help to give away the style's calligraphic roots. Humanist Serifs also tend to display a darker colour on the page in comparison with other later classifications when set as running text.

Jenson

OLD STYLE SERIF (GARALDE)

Old Styles date from the late fifteenth century onwards; they display similar visual characteristics to Humanist Serifs but their forms are less calligraphic. The group can be subdivided by nationality; the earliest Italian Old Styles (e.g. Bembo) date from the 1490s, French Old Styles (e.g. Garamond) date from the 1530s and tend to be slightly more refined, and Dutch Old Styles (e.g. Janson) date from the 1680s. The latter are often a little more condensed and have a slightly larger x-height. English Old Styles such as Caslon, which appeared in 1725, tend to be a little more sturdy than their predecessors.

Caslon

TRANSITIONAL SERIF

Dating from the early eighteenth century onwards, Transitional Serifs display few of the calligraphic qualities of their earlier counterparts. Details are finer across the board, with sharper symmetrical serifs and a more moderate and upright angle of stress that can vary from character to character. These qualities reflect the concurrent technological advances in paper and ink manufacture, which allowed the delicate letterforms to be reproduced cleanly and without significant distortion.

Baskerville

RATIONAL SERIF (DIDONE OR MODERN)

Dating from the late eighteenth century onwards, this classification, which contains the Didones or Moderns, is as far away from the Humanist Serif as one can get. Letterforms are 'drawn' more precisely rather than appearing to resemble handwritten forms, the stress angle is fully upright, and contrast is generally high with heavy vertical strokes meeting fine horizontal hairlines. Serifs are (not exclusively) unbracketed, and ball terminals are common.

Bodoni

FORMAL SCRIPT

Until the advent of digital typesetting technology, Script faces presented a problem for typesetters; they were difficult to letter space correctly because of the steeply angled stress and the overhanging details accompanying many characters. Today, the OpenType format and automatic glyph and ligature substitution mean sophisticated results are easily achievable. Formal Scripts closely resemble eighteenth-century calligraphic handwriting and copperplate engraving; they have a consistent angle of stress and high stroke contrast.

Bickham Script

CASUAL SCRIPT

Casual Scripts are the hand-lettered signs of the market, or the flamboyant advertising headlines created by pioneering Madison Avenue art directors in the 1920s and 1930s. The angle of stress and level of contrast between Casual Scripts can vary considerably, echoing the spontaneous hand-painted aspect of the style's origins. Generally speaking, Casual Scripts look as though they've been lettered with a brush and are highly calligraphic in nature.

The Carpenter

GROTESQUE SANS

When sans serif typefaces first began to appear in the early nineteenth century, people were unsure what to make of them and labelled them 'grotesque'. The term stuck and sans serif faces designed in the same style as the earliest examples are still referred to as Grotesque Sans. Characters display a moderate level of contrast with upright stress and are generally more complex than other sans serifs. Look for inward facing strokes and small apertures when identifying faces in this classification.

Folio

GROTESQUE SLAB (CLARENDON)

Dating from around the mid-nineteenth century, these heavyweight bruisers provide the very essence of the Victorian-era attention grabbing headline. Originally designed as Display faces, Grotesque Slab families that include a broader range of weights have appeared over the years, with some containing weights suitable for text setting. Serifs are bracketed and generally quite heavy, ball terminals are common, stress is upright and stroke contrast is moderate.

Clarendon

GEOMETRIC SLAB

Geometric Slabs share many of the characteristics of their sans serif counterparts; round characters are circular and stroke contrast is very low with little or no difference in the weight of the strokes and the consistently unbracketed serifs. Stress is distinctly vertical, adding to the general 'architectural' flavour of this classification. Although popular 1930s faces such as Memphis and Rockwell are seen as the original Geometric Slabs, they actually draw inspiration from an earlier face named Litho Antique, which appeared in 1910.

Archer

HUMANIST SLAB

Like Geometric Slabs, Humanist Slabs are very close in form to their sans serif counterparts. With a minimal amount of accommodating (and well-informed) adjustment, one could add unbracketed serifs to a Humanist Sans Serif typeface in order to create a reasonable facsimile of a Humanist Slab. However, they do generally feature a lower level of stroke contrast and good examples of this classification are far from being just simple adaptations.

PMN Caecilia

GOTHIC SANS

Gothic Sans typefaces are arguably closest to their Grotesque Sans (see page 92) counterparts in form but there are a few overall differences that set them apart. They retain the upright stress but are often simplified forms (e.g. a straight rather than curved leg on the 'R') with a lower contrast, a narrower body and an averagely larger x-height. Before the term sans serif entered common usage, 'Gothic' was used in the US to describe all sans serif typefaces.

Franklin Gothic

GEOMETRIC SANS

These are the most 'constructed' of all the sans serif classifications, displaying a precise geometry with round characters drawn as perfect circles and little or no stroke contrast. The most famous Geometric Sans, Futura, first appeared in 1927 and still sets a benchmark for typefaces that fall within this category. Ironically, perfect geometry isn't always the best friend of legibility, so contemporary Geometric Sans faces often include some optical adjustments to help improve readability at smaller point sizes.

Futura

HUMANIST SANS

Humanist Sans typefaces are the most calligraphic of all the sans serif classifications. Because of this they have a greater level of stroke contrast than their sans serif counterparts, but not quite as much as most serif faces. The heightened 'personality' of a Humanist Sans over other sans serifs mean they're arguably best suited to projects that need dynamic rather than understated typography. If you want the typeface to keep a low profile, this classification should be avoided. An identification clue is provided by the italic styles, which are often cursive or 'true italic' rather than a sloped roman.

Gill Sans

NEO-GROTESQUE SANS

The Neo-Grotesque Sans classification can be described as a pared down take on the Grotesque Sans style. The first of these, Folio, Univers and Helvetica (or Neue Haas Grotesk as it was originally named), first appeared in 1957 and the class is closely associated with the International Typographic Style (or Swiss Style) which flourished during the same period. Characters display very low contrast, stress is vertical and terminals are often horizontal. Because of their simple structure, Neo-Grotesque Sans faces work well at larger point sizes.

Neue Helvetica

NEO-HUMANIST SANS

This is a relatively new category that has appeared since the advent of digital technology. Typefaces designed in the last thirty or forty years often utilise and combine fresh ideas about the dynamics of the letterform, and it has become more common to encounter typefaces that defy precise classification under any present system. Neo-Humanist faces tend to follow a Humanist structure but have minimal stroke contrast, and large x-heights for improved readability at small sizes are normal.

Officina Sans

GLYPHIC (INSCRIBED)

The vast majority of serif typefaces are classified in part on the shapes of the strokes – some resemble pen strokes whilst others are more brush-like. However, characters can also be carved in stone or engraved in metal and it's this style of letterform that provides the basis for Glyphics, which can also be referred to as 'Inscribed'. Glyphics are distinguished by either tiny chiselled serifs, long elegant swashes and serifs or flared horizontal and vertical strokes.

Trajan

CONTEMPORARY SERIF

Like the new(ish) Neo-Humanist Sans category, the Contemporary Serif classification exists to accommodate new serif typeface designs that revive and/or combine ideas from existing styles that make it difficult to place them in one of the traditional groups. The incentive behind these fresh new designs is the improvement of typeface performance and legibility across all potential uses, which of course now includes screens. Contemporary Serifs often feature a large x-height, a relatively low stroke contrast and simplified detailing in the serifs and other terminals.

Neue Swift

DISPLAY

This is a difficult classification to pin down (in time as well as style, hence its appearance at the end of this sequence) as it can contain optically adjusted weights of other classifications. Broadly speaking it's exactly what it says it is – a class for any typeface that isn't intended for text setting. Many contemporary or updated typeface families contain specific optical weights for display usage with thinned down strokes which help to retain an even overall colour on the page. 'Novelty' faces can be dropped into this category as a kind of subset.

Bauhaus

Chapter 5

The Typefaces

JENSON

TYPE DESIGNER: Nicolas Jenson ¶ **FIRST APPEARANCE:** c.1470
CLASSIFICATION: Humanist Serif

USE FOR: Text that requires an historical yet characterful flavour

Jenson sits at the beginning of the story of all typefaces which use Latin or Roman letterforms. It was designed in Italy around 1470 by the French born punchcutter Nicolas Jenson after he opened his own print shop in Venice. Jenson had previously travelled to Mainz in Germany to learn about Gutenberg's new movable type technology and was well versed in the typographic arts. This is the first of the Humanist Serifs, which are also known as Venetian Serifs because of their geographic origin. The lowercase 'e' is an obvious indicator of the calligraphic influence that infuses every glyph; perhaps as a reflection of the methods followed by Gutenberg in Germany, typefaces at that time were designed to closely resemble popular handwriting styles. The accompanying italics that we see in contemporary versions of the face were of course added much later, and the latest OpenType version from Adobe reintroduces the extremely useful optical sizes utilised by older foundry type.

KEY FEATURES FOR CLASSIFICATION AND IDENTIFICATION

- Moderate contrast with a low x-height
- Angled stress
- Bracketed asymmetrical serifs are angled at the baseline
- Some glyphs feature a beak or spur

8/11 PT ADOBE JENSON REGULAR

LOREM IPSUM DOLOR SIT AMET, CONSECTETUER ADIPISCING ELIT, SED DIAM NONUMMY NIBH euismod tincidunt ut laoreet dolore magna aliquam erat volutpat. Ut wisi enim ad minim veniam, quis nostrud exerci tation ullamcorper suscipit lobortis nisl ut aliquip ex ea commodo consequat. Duis autem vel eum iriure dolor in hendrerit in vulputate velit esse molestie consequat, vel illum dolore eu feugiat nulla facilisis at vsero eros et accumsan et iusto odio dignissim qui blandit praesent luptatum zzril delenit augue duis dolore te feugait nulla facilisi. Nam liber tempor cum soluta nobis eleifend option congue nihil imperdiet doming id quod mazim placerat facer possim assum. Typi non habent

11/14 PT ADOBE JENSON REGULAR

UT WISI ENIM AD MINIM VENIAM, QUIS NOSTRUD EXERCI tation ullamcorper suscipit lobortis nisl ut aliquip ex ea commodo consequat. Duis autem vel eum iriure dolor in hendrerit in vulputate velit esse molestie consequat, vel illum dolore eu feugiat nulla facilisis at vero eros et accumsan et iusto odio dignissim qui blandit praesent luptatum zzril delenit augue duis dolore te feugait nulla

ADOBE JENSON ITALIC

abcdefghijklmnopqrstuvwxyz 1234567890
ABCDEFGHIJKLMNOPQRSTUVWXYZ

ADOBE JENSON CAPTION

abcdefghijklmnopqrstuvwxyz 1234567890
ABCDEFGHIJKLMNOPQRSTUVWXYZ

ADOBE JENSON SUBHEAD

abcdefghijklmnopqrstuvwxyz 1234567890
ABCDEFGHIJKLMNOPQRSTUVWXYZ

ADOBE JENSON SEMIBOLD

abcdefghijklmnopqrstuvwxyz 1234567890
ABCDEFGHIJKLMNOPQRSTUVWXYZ

ADOBE JENSON BOLD

abcdefghijklmnopqrstuvwxyz 1234567890
ABCDEFGHIJKLMNOPQRSTUVWXYZ

ADOBE JENSON REGULAR

abcdefghijklm
nopqrstuvwxyz
ABCDEFGHIJKLM
NOPQRSTUVWXYZ
1234567890 ¼ ½ ¾
[àóüßç](.,:;?!$€£&-*)
{ÀÓÜÇ}

BEMBO

Type designers: Aldus Manutius and Francesco Griffo
First appearance: 1495 ¶ **Classification:** Old Style Serif

Use for: Dense running text with historical or academic content

The Bembo we know today stems from the first commercial release of the typeface by Monotype in 1929. The foundry's principal typographic consultant, Stanley Morison, oversaw the design, modelling the glyphs closely on those first cut in Italy in 1495 by Francesco Griffo under the direction of the printer Aldus Manutius. It was Griffo's work which first began to move typeface design away from the familiar Humanist Serif towards a style that was less calligraphic and more refined. The fifteenth-century Bembo lacked an accompanying italic style (italics didn't make an appearance until Manutius introduced them a few years later) so Monotype based their contemporary version on the impressions of faces cut by Giovanni Taglienti and Ludovico Vincentino degli Arrighi in 1524 and 1526 respectively. Bembo offers a particularly good option for book designers setting large passages of dense running text, as the proportions of the letterforms create a very even colour on the page.

Key Features for Classification and Identification

- Moderate contrast and x-height
- Angled stress
- Small beak and flat bar on the 'e'
- Leg of the 'R' extends far beyond body

8/11 pt Bembo Regular
LOREM IPSUM DOLOR SIT AMET, CONSECTETUER ADIPISCING ELIT, SED DIAM NONUMMY NIBH euismod tincidunt ut laoreet dolore magna aliquam erat volutpat. Ut wisi enim ad minim veniam, quis nostrud exerci tation ullamcorper suscipit lobortis nisl ut aliquip ex ea commodo consequat. Duis autem vel eum iriure dolor in hendrerit in vulputate velit esse molestie consequat, vel illum dolore eu feugiat nulla facilisis at vsero eros et accumsan et iusto odio dignissim qui blandit praesent luptatum zzril delenit augue duis dolore te feugait nulla facilisi. Nam liber tempor cum soluta nobis eleifend option congue nihil imperdiet doming id quod mazim placerat facer

11/14 pt Bembo Regular
UT WISI ENIM AD MINIM VENIAM, QUIS NOSTRUD EXERCI tation ullamcorper suscipit lobortis nisl ut aliquip ex ea commodo consequat. Duis autem vel eum iriure dolor in hendrerit in vulputate velit esse molestie consequat, vel illum dolore eu feugiat nulla facilisis at vero eros et accumsan et iusto odio dignissim qui blandit praesent luptatum zzril delenit augue duis dolore te feugait

Bembo Italic

abcdefghijklmnopqrstuvwxyz 1234567890
ABCDEFGHIJKLMNOPQRSTUVWXYZ

Bembo Semibold

abcdefghijklmnopqrstuvwxyz 1234567890
ABCDEFGHIJKLMNOPQRSTUVWXYZ

Bembo Semibold Italic

abcdefghijklmnopqrstuvwxyz 1234567890
ABCDEFGHIJKLMNOPQRSTUVWXYZ

Bembo Bold

abcdefghijklmnopqrstuvwxyz 1234567890
ABCDEFGHIJKLMNOPQRSTUVWXYZ

Bembo Extra Bold

abcdefghijklmnopqrstuvwxyz 1234567890
ABCDEFGHIJKLMNOPQRSTUVWXYZ

Bembo Regular

abcdefghijklm
nopqrstuvwxyz
ABCDEFGHIJKLM
NOPQRSTUVWXYZ
1234567890 ¼ ½ ¾
[àóüßç](.,:;?!$€£&-★)
{ÀÓÜÇ}

GARAMOND

TYPE DESIGNERS: Claude Garamond and Robert Granjon
FIRST APPEARANCE: 1532 ¶ **CLASSIFICATION:** Old Style Serif

USE FOR: Adding an air of significance and knowingness to text

The earliest characters designed by the French punchcutter Claude Garamond date from the early sixteenth century and appear to have been heavily influenced by the work of Francesco Griffo (see page 102). Following a later 1540s commission from the French King Francis I, Garamond produced the typeface Grec du Roi (used for all printing carried out by the French court), and the design influenced the direction of typeface design throughout Western Europe. Because of the prolificacy of Garamond's particular style, linking contemporary typefaces to Garamond's original work can be problematic. It's only because of the exhaustive research carried out by Monotype's Beatrice Warde in the 1920s that we know several of Monotype's Garamond variants were in fact based on the work of Jean Jannon, another French punchcutter who worked some sixty years after Garamond's death. The open bowl of the 'P' and the serifs that terminate the bar of the 'T' are key identifiers.

KEY FEATURES FOR CLASSIFICATION AND IDENTIFICATION

- Moderate contrast with a relatively low x-height
- Angled stress
- Open bowls
- Counters and eyes are small

8/11 PT GARAMOND PREMIER REGULAR
LOREM IPSUM DOLOR SIT AMET, CONSECTETUER ADIPISCING ELIT, SED DIAM NONUMMY NIBH euismod tincidunt ut laoreet dolore magna aliquam erat volutpat. Ut wisi enim ad minim veniam, quis nostrud exerci tation ullamcorper suscipit lobortis nisl ut aliquip ex ea commodo consequat. Duis autem vel eum iriure dolor in hendrerit in vulputate velit esse molestie consequat, vel illum dolore eu feugiat nulla facilisis at vsero eros et accumsan et iusto odio dignissim qui blandit praesent luptatum zzril delenit augue duis dolore te feugait nulla facilisi. Nam liber tempor cum soluta nobis eleifend option congue nihil imperdiet doming id quod mazim placerat facer possim assum. Typi non habent claritatem insitam;

11/14 PT GARAMOND PREMIER REGULAR
UT WISI ENIM AD MINIM VENIAM, QUIS NOSTRUD EXERCI tation ullamcorper suscipit lobortis nisl ut aliquip ex ea commodo consequat. Duis autem vel eum iriure dolor in hendrerit in vulputate velit esse molestie consequat, vel illum dolore eu feugiat nulla facilisis at vero eros et accumsan et iusto odio dignissim qui blandit praesent luptatum zzril delenit augue duis dolore te feugait nulla facilisi.

GARAMOND PREMIER ITALIC

abcdefghijklmnopqrstuvwxyz 1234567890
ABCDEFGHIJKLMNOPQRSTUVWXYZ

GARAMOND PREMIER CAPTION

abcdefghijklmnopqrstuvwxyz 1234567890
ABCDEFGHIJKLMNOPQRSTUVWXYZ

GARAMOND PREMIER SUBHEAD

abcdefghijklmnopqrstuvwxyz 1234567890
ABCDEFGHIJKLMNOPQRSTUVWXYZ

GARAMOND PREMIER SEMIBOLD

abcdefghijklmnopqrstuvwxyz 1234567890
ABCDEFGHIJKLMNOPQRSTUVWXYZ

GARAMOND PREMIER BOLD

abcdefghijklmnopqrstuvwxyz 1234567890
ABCDEFGHIJKLMNOPQRSTUVWXYZ

GARAMOND PREMIER REGULAR

abcdefghijklm
nopqrstuvwxyz
ABCDEFGHIJKLM
NOPQRSTUVWXYZ
1234567890 ¼ ½ ¾
[àóüßç](.,:;?!$€£&-*)
{ÀÓÜÇ}

CASLON

Type designer: William Caslon ¶ **First appearance:** 1725
Classification: Old Style Serif

Use for: Practically anything requiring a serif typeface

At one time when typeface choice was far more limited than it is today, Caslon was considered by many printers to be the default. There was even a popular printer's moto; 'When in doubt, use Caslon.' William Caslon, a gunsmith and engraver, was one of the earliest English type founders to set up shop, opening his doors in 1716. He cut all his own punches, drawing on his existing skills as an engraver, and the 1725 typeface which bears his name was an instant success on a relatively global basis; for example, the original American Declaration of Independence is famously set in Caslon. Although classed as an Old Style Serif, Caslon is one of the first typefaces to move away from the Humanist form towards the more constructed Transitional style of faces such as Baskerville. For identification, look for the long tail of the 'Q', the horizontal bar of the otherwise calligraphic 'e' or the small extension of the stroke at the apex of the 'A'. The principal text elements in this book are set in Adobe Caslon.

Key Features for Classification and Identification

- Moderate contrast and x-height
- Near-vertical stress
- Stroke extends beyond apex of the 'A'
- Near-rectangular asymmetrical serifs with modest bracketing

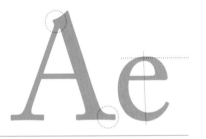

8/11 pt Adobe Caslon Regular
LOREM IPSUM DOLOR SIT AMET, CONSECTETUER ADIPISCING ELIT, SED DIAM NONUMMY NIBH euismod tincidunt ut laoreet dolore magna aliquam erat volutpat. Ut wisi enim ad minim veniam, quis nostrud exerci tation ullamcorper suscipit lobortis nisl ut aliquip ex ea commodo consequat. Duis autem vel eum iriure dolor in hendrerit in vulputate velit esse molestie consequat, vel illum dolore eu feugiat nulla facilisis at vsero eros et accumsan et iusto odio dignissim qui blandit praesent luptatum zzril delenit augue duis dolore te feugait nulla facilisi. Nam liber tempor cum soluta nobis eleifend option congue nihil imperdiet doming id quod mazim placerat facer

11/14 pt Adobe Caslon Regular
UT WISI ENIM AD MINIM VENIAM, QUIS NOSTRUD EXERCI tation ullamcorper suscipit lobortis nisl ut aliquip ex ea commodo consequat. Duis autem vel eum iriure dolor in hendrerit in vulputate velit esse molestie consequat, vel illum dolore eu feugiat nulla facilisis at vero eros et accumsan et iusto odio dignissim qui blandit praesent luptatum zzril delenit augue duis dolore te

ADOBE CASLON ITALIC

abcdefghijklmnopqrstuvwxyz 1234567890
ABCDEFGHIJKLMNOPQRSTUVWXYZ

ADOBE CASLON SEMIBOLD

abcdefghijklmnopqrstuvwxyz 1234567890
ABCDEFGHIJKLMNOPQRSTUVWXYZ

ADOBE CASLON SEMIBOLD ITALIC

abcdefghijklmnopqrstuvwxyz 1234567890
ABCDEFGHIJKLMNOPQRSTUVWXYZ

ADOBE CASLON BOLD

abcdefghijklmnopqrstuvwxyz 1234567890
ABCDEFGHIJKLMNOPQRSTUVWXYZ

ADOBE CASLON BOLD ITALIC

abcdefghijklmnopqrstuvwxyz 1234567890
ABCDEFGHIJKLMNOPQRSTUVWXYZ

ADOBE CASLON REGULAR

abcdefghijklm
nopqrstuvwxyz
ABCDEFGHIJKLM
NOPQRSTUVWXYZ
1234567890 ¼ ½ ¾
[àóüßç](.,:;?!$€£&-*)
{ÀÓÜÇ}

BASKERVILLE

TYPE DESIGNER: John Baskerville ¶ **FIRST APPEARANCE:** 1750s
CLASSIFICATION: Transitional Serif

USE FOR: Formal occasions and authoritative copy requiring gravitas

Baskerville is rightly regarded as the definitive eighteenth-century English Transitional serif, it being the first of its kind to be cut and manufactured in the United Kingdom. Driven by a desire to improve on the Old Style serif typefaces available at that time, the wealthy entrepreneur John Baskerville established a printing firm in Birmingham around 1750, employing the punchcutter John Handy to help him achieve his goal. Baskerville's own innovations in paper and ink manufacturing techniques, and his use of heated copper rollers to dry the ink more quickly during printing, meant he was able to cleanly reproduce his finely detailed letterforms without loss of quality. The type proved very popular, particularly in the American colonies, although some readers complained that the thinner strokes of the Transitional style 'hurt the eye…'. Widely available today from most digital foundries, look for the fine serifs and upright stress when distinguishing this Transitional Serif from Old Styles.

KEY FEATURES FOR CLASSIFICATION AND IDENTIFICATION

- Moderate contrast with a fairly large x-height
- Vertical stress
- Bracketed asymmetrical serifs
- Leg of the 'R' has a heavy, flat terminal

8/11 PT BASKERVILLE REGULAR

LOREM IPSUM DOLOR SIT AMET, CONSECTETUER ADIPISCING ELIT, sed diam nonummy nibh euismod tincidunt ut laoreet dolore magna aliquam erat volutpat. Ut wisi enim ad minim veniam, quis nostrud exerci tation ullamcorper suscipit lobortis nisl ut aliquip ex ea commodo consequat. Duis autem vel eum iriure dolor in hendrerit in vulputate velit esse molestie consequat, vel illum dolore eu feugiat nulla facilisis at vsero eros et accumsan et iusto odio dignissim qui blandit praesent luptatum zzril delenit augue duis dolore te feugait nulla facilisi. Nam liber tempor cum soluta nobis eleifend option congue nihil imperdiet doming id quod mazim placerat facer

11/14 PT BASKERVILLE REGULAR

UT WISI ENIM AD MINIM VENIAM, QUIS NOSTRUD EXERCI tation ullamcorper suscipit lobortis nisl ut aliquip ex ea commodo consequat. Duis autem vel eum iriure dolor in hendrerit in vulputate velit esse molestie consequat, vel illum dolore eu feugiat nulla facilisis at vero eros et accumsan et iusto odio dignissim qui blandit praesent luptatum zzril delenit augue duis dolore te feugait

Baskerville Italic

abcdefghijklmnopqrstuvwxyz 1234567890
ABCDEFGHIJKLMNOPQRSTUVWXYZ

Baskerville Semibold

abcdefghijklmnopqrstuvwxyz 1234567890
ABCDEFGHIJKLMNOPQRSTUVWXYZ

Baskerville Semibold Italic

abcdefghijklmnopqrstuvwxyz 1234567890
ABCDEFGHIJKLMNOPQRSTUVWXYZ

Baskerville Bold

abcdefghijklmnopqrstuvwxyz 1234567890
ABCDEFGHIJKLMNOPQRSTUVWXYZ

Baskerville Bold Italic

abcdefghijklmnopqrstuvwxyz 1234567890
ABCDEFGHIJKLMNOPQRSTUVWXYZ

Baskerville Regular

abcdefghijklm
nopqrstuvwxyz
ABCDEFGHIJKLM
NOPQRSTUVWXYZ
1234567890 ¼ ½ ¾
[àóüßç](.,:;?!$€£&-*)
{ÀÓÜÇ}

BODONI

TYPE DESIGNER: Giambatista Bodoni ¶ **FIRST APPEARANCE:** c.1790
CLASSIFICATION: Rational Serif

USE FOR: Fashionable subject matter and upmarket packaging

The Italian printer and typeface designer Giambattista Bodoni was a key
figure in the creation of the type classification known as Modern (which in
my preferred system sits within the overarching set of Rational Serifs).
Somewhat unusually Bodoni, who began working at the Vatican's *Propaganda
Fide* (Propagation of the Faith) printing house aged just eighteen, cut his own
punches and was immensely skilled in all areas of typeface design and
manufacture. An ardent admirer of John Baskerville (see page 108), Bodoni
made exquisitely elegant typefaces, typified by their very high stroke contrast,
fine hairline serifs and upright axis. Today there are many Bodoni revivals and
Bodoni-inspired faces available, but a 'classic' Bodoni-inspired typeface can
be spotted by looking closely at the serifs; an extremely subtle amount of
bracketing rather than an abrupt right angle at the stem indicates a design
that adheres more closely to Bodoni's original vision.

KEY FEATURES FOR CLASSIFICATION AND IDENTIFICATION

- Very high contrast with a moderate x-height
- Vertical stress
- Thin, flat, unbracketed serifs
- Ball terminals on some glyphs

8/11 PT BODONI BOOK
LOREM IPSUM DOLOR SIT AMET,
CONSECTETUER ADIPISCING ELIT,
SED DIAM NONUMMY NIBH EUISMOD
tincidunt ut laoreet dolore magna aliquam
erat volutpat. Ut wisi enim ad minim
veniam, quis nostrud exerci tation
ullamcorper suscipit lobortis nisl ut aliquip
ex ea commodo consequat. Duis autem vel
eum iriure dolor in hendrerit in vulputate
velit esse molestie consequat, vel illum
dolore eu feugiat nulla facilisis at vsero eros
et accumsan et iusto odio dignissim qui
blandit praesent luptatum zzril delenit
augue duis dolore te feugait nulla facilisi.
Nam liber tempor cum soluta nobis eleifend
option congue nihil imperdiet doming id
quod mazim placerat facer possim assum.

11/14 PT BODONI BOOK
UT WISI ENIM AD
MINIM VENIAM, QUIS
NOSTRUD EXERCI TATION
ullamcorper suscipit lobortis
nisl ut aliquip ex ea commodo
consequat. Duis autem vel eum
iriure dolor in hendrerit in
vulputate velit esse molestie
consequat, vel illum dolore eu
feugiat nulla facilisis at vero
eros et accumsan et iusto odio
dignissim qui blandit praesent
luptatum zzril delenit augue
duis dolore te feugait nulla

Bodoni Book

abcdefghijklmnopqrstuvwxyz 1234567890
ABCDEFGHIJKLMNOPQRSTUVWXYZ

Bodoni Book Italic

abcdefghijklmnopqrstuvwxyz 1234567890
ABCDEFGHIJKLMNOPQRSTUVWXYZ

Bodoni Italic

abcdefghijklmnopqrstuvwxyz 1234567890
ABCDEFGHIJKLMNOPQRSTUVWXYZ

Bodoni Bold

abcdefghijklmnopqrstuvwxyz 1234567890
ABCDEFGHIJKLMNOPQRSTUVWXYZ

Bodoni Bold Italic

abcdefghijklmnopqrstuvwxyz 1234567890
ABCDEFGHIJKLMNOPQRSTUVWXYZ

Bodoni Roman

abcdefghijklm
nopqrstuvwxyz
ABCDEFGHIJKLM
NOPQRSTUVWXYZ
1234567890 ¼½¾
[àóüßç](.,:;?!$€£&-*)
{ÀÓÜÇ}

CENTURY

TYPE DESIGNER: Linn Boyd Benton ¶ FIRST APPEARANCE: 1894
CLASSIFICATION: Rational Serif

USE FOR: Legible, closely packed text with an obvious sense of history

Today a large number of typefaces begin life as commissions from magazine publishers, but Century is possibly the first. Theodore L. De Vinne, the publisher of the US illustrated monthly *The Century*, was unhappy with the legibility of the existing font options at his disposal, particularly in relation to his older readers with poor eyesight. He requested a new typeface with good space-saving qualities and a darker colour on the page, and Linn Boyd Benton of American Type Founders was tasked with the design, which he completed in 1894. The initial range of weights was increased gradually by Benton's son, Morris Fuller Benton, after he too began working at ATF, and Century grew to become one the first 'type families', with a broad range of weights and styles. Don't confuse Century with Century Old Style or Century Schoolbook; both are related to the original Century but are quite different in terms of their contrast and overall metrics.

KEY FEATURES FOR CLASSIFICATION AND IDENTIFICATION

- Moderate contrast with a large x-height
- Vertical stress
- The leg of the 'R' has an upturned tail
- Large ball terminals on some glyphs

Ry

8/11 PT ITC CENTURY BOOK
LOREM IPSUM DOLOR SIT AMET, CONSECTETUER ADIPISCING ELIT, SED DIAM NONUMMY NIBH euismod tincidunt ut laoreet dolore magna aliquam erat volutpat. Ut wisi enim ad minim veniam, quis nostrud exerci tation ullamcorper suscipit lobortis nisl ut aliquip ex ea commodo consequat. Duis autem vel eum iriure dolor in hendrerit in vulputate velit esse molestie consequat, vel illum dolore eu feugiat nulla facilisis at vsero eros et accumsan et iusto odio dignissim qui blandit praesent luptatum zzril delenit augue duis dolore te feugait nulla facilisi. Nam liber tempor cum soluta nobis eleifend option

11/14 PT ITC CENTURY BOOK
UT WISI ENIM AD MINIM VENIAM, QUIS NOSTRUD EXERCI tation ullamcorper suscipit lobortis nisl ut aliquip ex ea commodo consequat. Duis autem vel eum iriure dolor in hendrerit in vulputate velit esse molestie consequat, vel illum dolore eu feugiat nulla facilisis at vero eros et accumsan et iusto odio dignissim qui blandit praesent luptatum

ITC Century Light

abcdefghijklmnopqrstuvwxyz 1234567890
ABCDEFGHIJKLMNOPQRSTUVWXYZ

ITC Century Light Italic

abcdefghijklmnopqrstuvwxyz 1234567890
ABCDEFGHIJKLMNOPQRSTUVWXYZ

ITC Century Book Italic

abcdefghijklmnopqrstuvwxyz 1234567890
ABCDEFGHIJKLMNOPQRSTUVWXYZ

ITC Century Bold

abcdefghijklmnopqrstuvwxyz 1234567890
ABCDEFGHIJKLMNOPQRSTUVWXYZ

ITC Century Ultra

abcdefghijklmnopqrstuvwxyz
1234567890 ABCDEFGHIJKLMNOPQ

ITC Century Book

abcdefghijklm
nopqrstuvwxyz
ABCDEFGHIJKLM
NOPQRSTUVWXYZ
1234567890 ¼ ½ ¾
[àóüßç](.,:;?!$€£&-*)
{ÀÓÜÇ}

COPPERPLATE GOTHIC

TYPE DESIGNER: Frederic W. Goudy ¶ **FIRST APPEARANCE:** 1901
CLASSIFICATION: Glyphic

USE FOR: Formal announcements and traditional calling cards

Copperplate Gothic was the first typeface released commercially by the newly formed American Type Founders. Completed in 1901, it was one of the prominent type designer Frederic W. Goudy's earliest efforts and carries the distinction of being the all-time best-seller of any ATF typeface. Despite its name, Copperplate Gothic isn't a gothic – it's a Glyphic and mimics the forms of letters carved in stone or metal. Its tiny serifs, a key element in the identification of this face, are so small that they almost disappear when the face is set at smaller point sizes. Although highly legible when set small, the typeface isn't really ideal for text setting (lowercase characters are substituted by small caps) and it only truly comes alive when set at larger display sizes. The coded naming system uses numbers to indicate weight and width, and letters (AB and BC) to indicate the relative height of the uppercase and small caps.

KEY FEATURES FOR CLASSIFICATION AND IDENTIFICATION

- Minimal contrast with a very large x-height
- Vertical stress
- Glyphic serifs mimic carved stone
- Lower case are small caps

8/11 PT COPPERPLATE GOTHIC 29 AB
LOREM IPSUM DOLOR SIT AMET, CONSECTETUER ADIPISCING ELIT, SED DIAM NONUMMY NIBH EUISMOD TINCIDUNT UT LAOREET DOLORE MAGNA ALIQUAM ERAT VOLUTPAT. UT WISI ENIM AD MINIM VENIAM, QUIS NOSTRUD EXERCI TATION ULLAMCORPER SUSCIPIT LOBORTIS NISL UT ALIQUIP EX EA COMMODO CONSEQUAT. DUIS AUTEM VEL EUM IRIURE DOLOR IN HENDRERIT IN VULPUTATE VELIT ESSE MOLESTIE CONSEQUAT, VEL ILLUM DOLORE EU FEUGIAT NULLA FACILISIS AT VSERO EROS ET ACCUMSAN ET IUSTO ODIO DIGNISSIM QUI BLANDIT PRAESENT LUPTATUM ZZRIL DELENIT AUGUE DUIS DOLORE TE FEUGAIT NULLA FACILISI.

11/14 PT COPPERPLATE GOTHIC 29 AB
UT WISI ENIM AD MINIM VENIAM, QUIS NOSTRUD EXERCI TATION ULLAMCORPER SUSCIPIT LOBORTIS NISL UT ALIQUIP EX EA COMMODO CONSEQUAT. DUIS AUTEM VEL EUM IRIURE DOLOR IN HENDRERIT IN VULPUTATE VELIT ESSE MOLESTIE CONSEQUAT, VEL ILLUM DOLORE EU FEUGIAT NULLA FACILISIS AT VERO EROS ET ACCUMSAN ET IUSTO ODIO

Copperplate Gothic 30 AB

ABCDEFGHIJKLMNOPQRSTUVWXYZ 1234567890
ABCDEFGHIJKLMNOPQRSTUVWXYZ

Copperplate Gothic 31 AB

ABCDEFGHIJKLMNOPQRSTUVWXYZ
1234567890 ABCDEFGHIJKLMN

Copperplate Gothic 32 AB

ABCDEFGHIJKLMNOPQRSTUVWXYZ
1234567890 ABCDEFGHIJKLMN

Copperplate Gothic 29 BC

ABCDEFGHIJKLMNOPQRSTUVWXYZ 1234567890
ABCDEFGHIJKLMNOPQRSTUVWXYZ

Copperplate Gothic 33 BC

ABCDEFGHIJKLMNOPQRSTUVWXYZ
1234567890 ABCDEFGHIJKLMNOPQRST

Copperplate Gothic 29 AB

ABCDEFGHIJKLM
NOPQRSTUVWXYZ
ABCDEFGHIJKLM
NOPQRSTUVWXYZ
1234567890 ¼ ½ ¾
[ÀÓÜSSÇ](.,:;?!$€£&-*)
{ÀÓÜÇ}

GOUDY OLD STYLE

TYPE DESIGNER: Frederic W. Goudy ¶ **FIRST APPEARANCE:** 1915–1916
CLASSIFICATION: Old Style Serif

USE FOR: Elegant, flowing text that has some room to breathe

Goudy Old Style, perhaps the best-known typeface of the many designed by the prolific Frederic W. Goudy for American Type Founders, is classed as an Old Style Serif but it also displays traits typical of sixteenth-century Humanist Serifs. The lower arm of the uppercase 'E' has a distinctive calligraphic flow to it and provides a useful identifier for this typeface. In some ways this is hardly surprising as Goudy was interested in calligraphy from an early age and began his design career as a freelance lettering artist. Goudy was at times famously grumpy and disliked the way ATF interfered in his creative process. Despite the long-term success of his typeface, he was once quoted as saying, 'I am almost satisfied that the design is a good one, marred only by the short descenders which I allowed the American Type Founders to inveigle me into giving p, q, g, j and y – though only under protest.'

KEY FEATURES FOR CLASSIFICATION AND IDENTIFICATION

- Moderate contrast and x-height
- Steeply angled stress
- Diamond shaped dots or tittles
- Bracketed serifs are asymmetrical

8/11 PT GOUDY OLD STYLE REGULAR
LOREM IPSUM DOLOR SIT AMET, CONSECTETUER ADIPISCING ELIT, SED DIAM NONUMMY NIBH euismod tincidunt ut laoreet dolore magna aliquam erat volutpat. Ut wisi enim ad minim veniam, quis nostrud exerci tation ullamcorper suscipit lobortis nisl ut aliquip ex ea commodo consequat. Duis autem vel eum iriure dolor in hendrerit in vulputate velit esse molestie consequat, vel illum dolore eu feugiat nulla facilisis at vsero eros et accumsan et iusto odio dignissim qui blandit praesent luptatum zzril delenit augue duis dolore te feugait nulla facilisi. Nam liber tempor cum soluta nobis eleifend option congue nihil imperdiet doming id quod mazim placerat facer

11/14 PT GOUDY OLD STYLE REGULAR
UT WISI ENIM AD MINIM VENIAM, QUIS NOSTRUD EXERCI tation ullamcorper suscipit lobortis nisl ut aliquip ex ea commodo consequat. Duis autem vel eum iriure dolor in hendrerit in vulputate velit esse molestie consequat, vel illum dolore eu feugiat nulla facilisis at vero eros et accumsan et iusto odio dignissim qui blandit praesent luptatum zzril delenit augue

GOUDY OLD STYLE ITALIC

abcdefghijklmnopqrstuvwxyz 1234567890
ABCDEFGHIJKLMNOPQRSTUVWXYZ

GOUDY OLD STYLE BOLD

abcdefghijklmnopqrstuvwxyz 1234567890
ABCDEFGHIJKLMNOPQRSTUVWXYZ

GOUDY OLD STYLE BOLD ITALIC

abcdefghijklmnopqrstuvwxyz 1234567890
ABCDEFGHIJKLMNOPQRSTUVWXYZ

GOUDY OLD STYLE REGULAR

abcdefghijklm

nopqrstuvwxyz

ABCDEFGHIJKLM

NOPQRSTUVWXYZ

1234567890 ¼ ½ ¾

[àóüßç](.,:;?!$€£&-*)

{ÀÓÜÇ}

PERPETUA

TYPE DESIGNER: Eric Gill ¶ **FIRST APPEARANCE:** 1925–1932
CLASSIFICATION: Transitional Serif

USE FOR: Authoritative text and an extra twist of personality

In 1925 Stanley Morison, the principal typographic consultant at Monotype, decided to commission a fresh serif face for the foundry and approached Eric Gill (see page 120). In order to keep the process as traditionally pure as possible, Morison selected a French punchcutter named Charles Malin to make actual punches for the manufacture of the matrices, but unfortunately Gill wasn't entirely happy with the end results. It ultimately fell to the staff overseen by Frank Hinman Pierpont at Monotype's Salfords works to tie up the loose ends, and Perpetua finally saw the light of day in 1928 as the text face in a limited edition book named *The Passion of Perpetua and Felicity*. An italic designed to accompany Perpetua was released separately and originally named Felicity, but was later renamed Perpetua Italic. The typeface is far closer to a Transitional Serif than Gill's other serif face Joanna, with the typical sharp bracketed serifs and relatively high contrast one would expect to see.

KEY FEATURES FOR CLASSIFICATION AND IDENTIFICATION

- Fairly high contrast with a moderate x-height
- Vertical stress
- Prominent, precisely curved brackets
- Clean-cut, tapered finials

Ma

8/11 PT PERPETUA REGULAR
LOREM IPSUM DOLOR SIT AMET, CONSECTETUER ADIPISCING ELIT, SED DIAM NONUMMY NIBH EUISMOD tincidunt ut laoreet dolore magna aliquam erat volutpat. Ut wisi enim ad minim veniam, quis nostrud exerci tation ullamcorper suscipit lobortis nisl ut aliquip ex ea commodo consequat. Duis autem vel eum iriure dolor in hendrerit in vulputate velit esse molestie consequat, vel illum dolore eu feugiat nulla facilisis at vsero eros et accumsan et iusto odio dignissim qui blandit praesent luptatum zzril delenit augue duis dolore te feugait nulla facilisi. Nam liber tempor cum soluta nobis eleifend option congue nihil imperdiet doming id quod mazim placerat facer possim assum. Typi non habent claritatem insitam; est usus legentis in iis

11/14 PT PERPETUA REGULAR
UT WISI ENIM AD MINIM VENIAM, QUIS NOSTRUD EXERCI tation ullamcorper suscipit lobortis nisl ut aliquip ex ea commodo consequat. Duis autem vel eum iriure dolor in hendrerit in vulputate velit esse molestie consequat, vel illum dolore eu feugiat nulla facilisis at vero eros et accumsan et iusto odio dignissim qui blandit praesent luptatum zzril delenit augue duis dolore te feugait nulla facilisi. Nam liber

PERPETUA ITALIC

abcdefghijklmnopqrstuvwxyz 1234567890
ABCDEFGHIJKLMNOPQRSTUVWXYZ

PERPETUA BOLD

abcdefghijklmnopqrstuvwxyz 1234567890
ABCDEFGHIJKLMNOPQRSTUVWXYZ

PERPETUA BOLD ITALIC

abcdefghijklmnopqrstuvwxyz 1234567890
ABCDEFGHIJKLMNOPQRSTUVWXYZ

PERPETUA REGULAR

abcdefghijklm

nopqrstuvwxyz

ABCDEFGHIJKLM

NOPQRSTUVWXYZ

1234567890 ¼ ½ ¾

[àóüßç](.,:;?!$€£&-*)

{ÀÓÜÇ}

JOANNA

Type designer: Eric Gill ¶ **First appearance:** 1930
Classification: Transitional Serif

Use for: An engineered quality to formal seriffed typesetting

The famous (and controversial) designer, printer and stone carver Eric Gill designed Joanna as the house-typeface for a joint venture, the ill-fated printing firm Hague & Gill, which he established with his son-in-law René Hague in 1930. The face is named after his daughter Joanna. Reports suggest that the face was a personal favourite of Gill's; he considered it a 'type with no frills' and infused it with an appealing and, at the time, relatively unique engineered quality. This comes in part from the fact that structurally it's a Transitional Serif but it has unbracketed serifs, something which singles Joanna out for easy identification. The italic weights are also unusual because they take the form of a sloped roman but some characters, the 'a', 'e' and 'g', are cursive. Hague & Gill was not a success and the type was sold on, eventually finding its way to a commercial release by Monotype in 1958. In 2015, Monotype released Joanna Nova, an extensive update with a total of nine separate weights.

Key Features for Classification and Identification

- Fairly low contrast with a moderate x-height
- Vertical stress
- Flat, horizontal, unbracketed serifs
- Bowls flatten at baseline

8/11 pt Joanna Regular
LOREM IPSUM DOLOR SIT AMET, CONSECTETUER ADIPISCING ELIT, SED DIAM NONUMMY NIBH EUISMOD tincidunt ut laoreet dolore magna aliquam erat volutpat. Ut wisi enim ad minim veniam, quis nostrud exerci tation ullamcorper suscipit lobortis nisl ut aliquip ex ea commodo consequat. Duis autem vel eum iriure dolor in hendrerit in vulputate velit esse molestie consequat, vel illum dolore eu feugiat nulla facilisis at vsero eros et accumsan et iusto odio dignissim qui blandit praesent luptatum zzril delenit augue duis dolore te feugait nulla facilisi. Nam liber tempor cum soluta nobis eleifend option congue nihil imperdiet doming id quod mazim placerat facer

11/14 pt Joanna Regular
UT WISI ENIM AD MINIM VENIAM, QUIS NOSTRUD EXERCI tation ullamcorper suscipit lobortis nisl ut aliquip ex ea commodo consequat. Duis autem vel eum iriure dolor in hendrerit in vulputate velit esse molestie consequat, vel illum dolore eu feugiat nulla facilisis at vero eros et accumsan et iusto odio dignissim qui blandit praesent luptatum zzril delenit augue duis dolore te feugait

JOANNA ITALIC

abcdefghijklmnopqrstuvwxyz 1234567890
ABCDEFGHIJKLMNOPQRSTUVWXYZ

JOANNA SEMIBOLD

abcdefghijklmnopqrstuvwxyz 1234567890
ABCDEFGHIJKLMNOPQRSTUVWXYZ

JOANNA SEMIBOLD ITALIC

abcdefghijklmnopqrstuvwxyz 1234567890
ABCDEFGHIJKLMNOPQRSTUVWXYZ

JOANNA BOLD

abcdefghijklmnopqrstuvwxyz 1234567890
ABCDEFGHIJKLMNOPQRSTUVWXYZ

JOANNA EXTRA BOLD

abcdefghijklmnopqrstuvwxyz 1234567890
ABCDEFGHIJKLMNOPQRSTUVWXYZ

JOANNA REGULAR

abcdefghijklm
nopqrstuvwxyz
ABCDEFGHIJKLM
NOPQRSTUVWXYZ
1234567890 ¼ ½ ¾
[àóüßç](.,:;?!$€£&-*)
{ÀÓÜÇ}

TIMES NEW ROMAN

Type designers: Stanley Morison and Victor Lardent
First appearance: 1932 ¶ **Classification:** Transitional Serif

Use for: Official text that needs to maintain its neutrality

Everyone knows Times New Roman – it's everywhere, the seriffed equivalent of Helvetica or Arial. Non-designers with no knowledge of typography regularly refer to all seriffed typefaces as 'Times fonts', it's that ubiquitous. Because of this, many professional designers dismiss it as unusable, which is frankly a shame as it's an attractive and highly legible typeface. Designed by Monotype's Stanley Morison and drawn by Victor Lardent, a draughtsman at *The Times* newspaper, the typeface was conceived as part of an early 1930s modernization of the existing look of the newspaper aimed at improving legibility and saving space. It's inspired by Plantin, a sixteenth-century Old Style by Robert Granjon, but Morison's sharpened details and increased contrast created a face that's very much a Transitional Serif. It first appeared in *The Times* on 3 October 1932, and was used unchanged for forty years. All new typefaces used by the paper since 1972 have been based on the original design of Times New Roman.

Key Features for Classification and Identification

- High contrast with a fairly large x-height
- Angled stress
- Serifs feature sharply curved brackets
- Apertures are small

8/11 pt Times New Roman Regular
LOREM IPSUM DOLOR SIT AMET, CONSECTETUER ADIPISCING ELIT, SED DIAM NONUMMY NIBH euismod tincidunt ut laoreet dolore magna aliquam erat volutpat. Ut wisi enim ad minim veniam, quis nostrud exerci tation ullamcorper suscipit lobortis nisl ut aliquip ex ea commodo consequat. Duis autem vel eum iriure dolor in hendrerit in vulputate velit esse molestie consequat, vel illum dolore eu feugiat nulla facilisis at vsero eros et accumsan et iusto odio dignissim qui blandit praesent luptatum zzril delenit augue duis dolore te feugait nulla facilisi. Nam liber tempor cum soluta nobis eleifend option congue nihil imperdiet

11/14 pt Times New Roman Regular
UT WISI ENIM AD MINIM VENIAM, QUIS NOSTRUD EXERCI tation ullamcorper suscipit lobortis nisl ut aliquip ex ea commodo consequat. Duis autem vel eum iriure dolor in hendrerit in vulputate velit esse molestie consequat, vel illum dolore eu feugiat nulla facilisis at vero eros et accumsan et iusto odio dignissim qui blandit praesent luptatum zzril

Times New Roman Italic

abcdefghijklmnopqrstuvwxyz 1234567890
ABCDEFGHIJKLMNOPQRSTUVWXYZ

Times New Roman Bold

abcdefghijklmnopqrstuvwxyz 1234567890
ABCDEFGHIJKLMNOPQRSTUVWXYZ

Times New Roman Bold Italic

abcdefghijklmnopqrstuvwxyz 1234567890
ABCDEFGHIJKLMNOPQRSTUVWXYZ

Times New Roman Condensed

abcdefghijklmnopqrstuvwxyz 1234567890
ABCDEFGHIJKLMNOPQRSTUVWXYZ

Times New Roman Bold Condensed

abcdefghijklmnopqrstuvwxyz 1234567890
ABCDEFGHIJKLMNOPQRSTUVWXYZ

Times New Roman Regular

abcdefghijklm
nopqrstuvwxyz
ABCDEFGHIJKLM
NOPQRSTUVWXYZ
1234567890 ¼ ½ ¾
[àóüßç](.,:;?!$€£&-*)
{ÀÓÜÇ}

SABON

TYPE DESIGNER: Jan Tschichold ¶ **FIRST APPEARANCE:** 1964–1967
CLASSIFICATION: Old Style Serif

USE FOR: Precise text setting that's sharper than the average serif

Sabon was designed between 1964 and 1967 by the well-known designer and typographer Jan Tschichold as part of a joint commission from Monotype, Linotype and the Stempel Type Foundry in Frankfurt. The challenging brief required a brand new serif typeface that could retain its form when set mechanically in metal on both the Monotype and Linotype systems, and by hand using traditional foundry type. Tschichold solved the problem by designing both the roman and bold weights so they occupied exactly the same width. Sabon continued to blaze a trail as one of the first typefaces to reach the digital platform in 1980, and whilst it's an Old Style Serif, it shouldn't be considered a Garamond revival as some might have you believe. There's far more to Sabon than that – it's a fully rethought adaptation of an Old Style with some clever things going on under the hood. A contemporary revival, Sabon Next, expands the family from four to six weights and was released in 2002.

KEY FEATURES FOR CLASSIFICATION AND IDENTIFICATION

- Moderate contrast and x-height
- Angled stress
- Bracketed serifs are slightly asymmetric
- Open bowls

8/11 PT SABON ROMAN
LOREM IPSUM DOLOR SIT AMET, CONSECTETUER ADIPISCING ELIT, SED DIAM NONUMMY NIBH euismod tincidunt ut laoreet dolore magna aliquam erat volutpat. Ut wisi enim ad minim veniam, quis nostrud exerci tation ullamcorper suscipit lobortis nisl ut aliquip ex ea commodo consequat. Duis autem vel eum iriure dolor in hendrerit in vulputate velit esse molestie consequat, vel illum dolore eu feugiat nulla facilisis at vsero eros et accumsan et iusto odio dignissim qui blandit praesent luptatum zzril delenit augue duis dolore te feugait nulla facilisi. Nam liber tempor cum soluta nobis eleifend option congue nihil

11/14 PT SABON ROMAN
UT WISI ENIM AD MINIM VENIAM, QUIS NOSTRUD EXERCI tation ullamcorper suscipit lobortis nisl ut aliquip ex ea commodo consequat. Duis autem vel eum iriure dolor in hendrerit in vulputate velit esse molestie consequat, vel illum dolore eu feugiat nulla facilisis at vero eros et accumsan et iusto odio dignissim qui blandit praesent luptatum zzril

SABON ITALIC

abcdefghijklmnopqrstuvwxyz 1234567890
ABCDEFGHIJKLMNOPQRSTUVWXYZ

SABON BOLD

abcdefghijklmnopqrstuvwxyz 1234567890
ABCDEFGHIJKLMNOPQRSTUVWXYZ

SABON BOLD ITALIC

abcdefghijklmnopqrstuvwxyz 1234567890
ABCDEFGHIJKLMNOPQRSTUVWXYZ

SABON ROMAN

abcdefghijklm
nopqrstuvwxyz
ABCDEFGHIJKLM
NOPQRSTUVWXYZ
1234567890 ¼ ½ ¾
[àóüßç](.,:;?!$€£&-*)
{ÀÓÜÇ}

SWIFT (NEUE SWIFT)

TYPE DESIGNER: Gerard Unger ¶ **FIRST APPEARANCE:** 1985–2009
CLASSIFICATION: Contemporary Serif

USE FOR: Making everyday text look more interesting on the page

The developmental period of Swift is lengthy; the Dutch designer Gerard Unger designed the original version of this Contemporary Serif in 1985 for use in the notoriously difficult printing environment of newspaper publishing. The chunky wedge serifs, the large x-height, the open apertures and the sturdy overall form of the glyphs help the characters retain their shapes when printed at high speed on low quality paper stock. A 1995 update named Swift 2.0 was released, and by 2009 an OpenType family of five separate weights replaced all previous versions. The face has enjoyed significant popularity outside its intended area of use and remains a favourite of magazine and book designers. The prominent serifs and blunt, wedge-shaped terminals on characters such as the 'f' and 'r' are key indicators for identification, and it's these very features that provide the aesthetic which gives this typeface its edge.

KEY FEATURES FOR CLASSIFICATION AND IDENTIFICATION

- Moderate contrast with a large x-height
- Slightly angled stress
- Large serifs are wedge-shaped
- Arched strokes taper dramatically

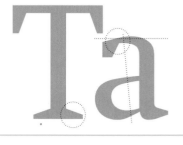

8/11 PT NEUE SWIFT REGULAR
LOREM IPSUM DOLOR SIT AMET, CONSECTETUER ADIPISCING ELIT, SED DIAM NONUMMY NIBH euismod tincidunt ut laoreet dolore magna aliquam erat volutpat. Ut wisi enim ad minim veniam, quis nostrud exerci tation ullamcorper suscipit lobortis nisl ut aliquip ex ea commodo consequat. Duis autem vel eum iriure dolor in hendrerit in vulputate velit esse molestie consequat, vel illum dolore eu feugiat nulla facilisis at vsero eros et accumsan et iusto odio dignissim qui blandit praesent luptatum zzril delenit augue duis dolore te feugait nulla facilisi. Nam liber tempor cum soluta nobis eleifend

11/14 PT NEUE SWIFT REGULAR
UT WISI ENIM AD MINIM VENIAM, QUIS NOSTRUD EXERCI tation ullamcorper suscipit lobortis nisl ut aliquip ex ea commodo consequat. Duis autem vel eum iriure dolor in hendrerit in vulputate velit esse molestie consequat, vel illum dolore eu feugiat nulla facilisis at vero eros et accumsan et iusto odio dignissim qui blandit praesent luptatum

Neue Swift Light

abcdefghijklmnopqrstuvwxyz 1234567890
ABCDEFGHIJKLMNOPQRSTUVWXYZ

Neue Swift Italic

abcdefghijklmnopqrstuvwxyz 1234567890
ABCDEFGHIJKLMNOPQRSTUVWXYZ

Neue Swift Book

abcdefghijklmnopqrstuvwxyz 1234567890
ABCDEFGHIJKLMNOPQRSTUVWXYZ

Neue Swift Semibold

abcdefghijklmnopqrstuvwxyz 1234567890
ABCDEFGHIJKLMNOPQRSTUVWXYZ

Neue Swift Bold

abcdefghijklmnopqrstuvwxyz 1234567890
ABCDEFGHIJKLMNOPQRSTUVWXYZ

Neue Swift regular

abcdefghijklm
nopqrstuvwxyz
ABCDEFGHIJKLM
NOPQRSTUVWXYZ
1234567890 ¼ ½ ¾
[àóüßç](.,:;?!$€£&-*)
{ÀÓÜÇ}

BRIOSO

Type designer: Robert Slimbach ¶ **First appearance:** 2003
Classification: Humanist Serif

Use for: Poetic licence and subject matter of a hand-crafted nature

Robert Slimbach's 2003 typeface Brioso (Italian for 'lively') is something of a triumph as it manages to be a *very* calligraphic Humanist Serif while working simultaneously as a legible text face. If it were any more calligraphic it would become a script, but Slimbach has managed to blend the two styles very successfully, creating a contemporary text family with no less than forty-two separate styles. In recent years, typeface designers have once again begun to introduce optical sizing (see page 58) to typeface families and Brioso is no exception with four optical sizes included; caption, text, subhead and display. Although there are clear comparisons with early Humanist Serifs like Jenson in the forms of the characters (look at the 'e' in particular) the design is very personal to Slimbach, who is an accomplished calligrapher in his own right. The final glyphs are created from a series of alphabets drawn by Slimbach, resulting in a digital version of his own hand lettering style.

Key Features for Classification and Identification

- Fairly high contrast with a moderate x-height
- Angled stress
- Calligraphic letterforms
- Some glyphs feature a beak or spur

8/11 pt Brioso Regular

LOREM IPSUM DOLOR SIT AMET, CONSECTETUER ADIPISCING ELIT, SED DIAM NONUMMY NIBH euismod tincidunt ut laoreet dolore magna aliquam erat volutpat. Ut wisi enim ad minim veniam, quis nostrud exerci tation ullamcorper suscipit lobortis nisl ut aliquip ex ea commodo consequat. Duis autem vel eum iriure dolor in hendrerit in vulputate velit esse molestie consequat, vel illum dolore eu feugiat nulla facilisis at vsero eros et accumsan et iusto odio dignissim qui blandit praesent luptatum zzril delenit augue duis dolore te feugait nulla facilisi. Nam liber tempor cum soluta nobis eleifend option congue nihil imperdiet doming id quod mazim placerat facer possim assum.

11/14 pt Brioso Regular

UT WISI ENIM AD MINIM VENIAM, QUIS NOSTRUD EXERCI tation ullamcorper suscipit lobortis nisl ut aliquip ex ea commodo consequat. Duis autem vel eum iriure dolor in hendrerit in vulputate velit esse molestie consequat, vel illum dolore eu feugiat nulla facilisis at vero eros et accumsan et iusto odio dignissim qui blandit praesent luptatum zzril delenit augue duis dolore te feugait

Brioso Italic

abcdefghijklmnopqrstuvwxyz 1234567890
ABCDEFGHIJKLMNOPQRSTUVWXYZ

Brioso Caption

abcdefghijklmnopqrstuvwxyz 1234567890
ABCDEFGHIJKLMNOPQRSTUVWXYZ

Brioso Subhead

abcdefghijklmnopqrstuvwxyz 1234567890
ABCDEFGHIJKLMNOPQRSTUVWXYZ

Brioso Semibold

abcdefghijklmnopqrstuvwxyz 1234567890
ABCDEFGHIJKLMNOPQRSTUVWXYZ

Brioso Bold

abcdefghijklmnopqrstuvwxyz 1234567890
ABCDEFGHIJKLMNOPQRSTUVWXYZ

Brioso Regular

abcdefghijklm
nopqrstuvwxyz
ABCDEFGHIJKLM
NOPQRSTUVWXYZ
1234567890 ¼ ½ ¾
[àóüßç](.,:;?!$€£&-*)
{ÀÓÜÇ}

CLARENDON

TYPE DESIGNER: Robert Besley ¶ **FIRST APPEARANCE:** 1845
CLASSIFICATION: Grotesque Slab

USE FOR: Creating a Victorian-era look for historical design projects

Clarendon is a sub-classification all of its own, falling within the larger Grotesque Slab group. The original Clarendon dates from 1845 and was designed in London by Robert Besley for R. Besley & Co., previously the Fann Street Foundry. The face was incredibly popular when it first appeared and today it conjures the look of the Victorian-era poster perfectly. It was the first ever typeface to be patented, but the patent only lasted for three years and other foundries were quick to release their own versions. Weights were originally very limited and had no accompanying italic styles, but more recent versions such as that from URW++ (used on this spread) carry additional weights and add oblique roman italics. Sentinel from Hoefler & Co., although a completely different typeface, offers an excellent alternative choice. Key visual pointers are provided by the heavy bracketed serifs and the prominent ball terminals, and the 'Q', 'R' and 'a' are useful identifiers.

KEY FEATURES FOR CLASSIFICATION AND IDENTIFICATION

- Moderate contrast with a large x-height
- Vertical stress
- 'Q', 'R' and 'a' have upturned tails
- Heavy, bracketed serifs

8/11 PT CLARENDON REGULAR
LOREM IPSUM DOLOR SIT AMET, CONSECTETUER ADIPISCING ELIT, SED DIAM NONUMMY nibh euismod tincidunt ut laoreet dolore magna aliquam erat volutpat. Ut wisi enim ad minim veniam, quis nostrud exerci tation ullamcorper suscipit lobortis nisl ut aliquip ex ea commodo consequat. Duis autem vel eum iriure dolor in hendrerit in vulputate velit esse molestie consequat, vel illum dolore eu feugiat nulla facilisis at vsero eros et accumsan et iusto odio dignissim qui blandit praesent luptatum zzril delenit augue duis

11/14 PT CLARENDON REGULAR
UT WISI ENIM AD MINIM VENIAM, QUIS NOSTRUD EXERCI tation ullamcorper suscipit lobortis nisl ut aliquip ex ea commodo consequat. Duis autem vel eum iriure dolor in hendrerit in vulputate velit esse molestie consequat, vel illum dolore eu feugiat nulla facilisis at vero eros et accumsan et iusto odio

CLARENDON LIGHT

abcdefghijklmnopqrstuvwxyz 012345678
ABCDEFGHIJKLMNOPQRSTUVWXYZ

CLARENDON REGULAR OBLIQUE

abcdefghijklmnopqrstuvwxyz 012345678
ABCDEFGHIJKLMNOPQRSTUVWXYZ

CLARENDON MEDIUM

abcdefghijklmnopqrstuvwxyz 012345678
ABCDEFGHIJKLMNOPQRSTUVWXYZ

CLARENDON BOLD

abcdefghijklmnopqrstuvwxyz 01234567
ABCDEFGHIJKLMNOPQRSTUVWXYZ

CLARENDON EXTRA BOLD

abcdefghijklmnopqrstuvwxyz
0123456789 ABCDEFGHIJKLMNOPQR

CLARENDON REGULAR

abcdefghijklm
nopqrstuvwxyz
ABCDEFGHIJKLM
NOPQRSTUVWXYZ
1234567890 ¼ ½ ¾
[àóüßç](.,:;?!$€£&-*)
{ÀÓÜÇ}

ROCKWELL

TYPE DESIGNERS: Monotype ¶ **FIRST APPEARANCE:** 1933–1934
CLASSIFICATION: Geometric Slab

USE FOR: A retro feel that other Geometric Slabs can't deliver

In real terms Rockwell began life in 1910 as a typeface named Litho Antique, issued by the Inland Type Foundry of St Louis. American Type Founders purchased the foundry and its typefaces in 1911 and some years later in 1931 issued a revival which was renamed Rockwell Antique, then simply Rockwell after a further revision made between 1933–1934. Another typeface, Stymie, emerged around the same time because of a misunderstanding at Monotype and is very similar indeed to Rockwell but not identical, so beware of easy misidentification between these two faces. It's possibly because of its earlier origins that Rockwell has a slightly softer feel than other Geometric Slabs; the double-storey 'a' and the round dots of the 'i' and 'j' are atypical of other comparable faces such as Memphis and give Rockwell a more antiquated or handmade feel. The aforementioned lowercase 'a' is a useful character for identification.

KEY FEATURES FOR CLASSIFICATION AND IDENTIFICATION

- Minimal contrast with a moderate x-height
- Vertical stress
- Regular weight is quite heavy
- Some serifs are one-sided

Gh

8/11 PT ROCKWELL REGULAR
LOREM IPSUM DOLOR SIT AMET, CONSECTETUER ADIPISCING ELIT, SED DIAM NONUMMY NIBH euismod tincidunt ut laoreet dolore magna aliquam erat volutpat. Ut wisi enim ad minim veniam, quis nostrud exerci tation ullamcorper suscipit lobortis nisl ut aliquip ex ea commodo consequat. Duis autem vel eum iriure dolor in hendrerit in vulputate velit esse molestie consequat, vel illum dolore eu feugiat nulla facilisis at vsero eros et accumsan et iusto odio dignissim qui blandit praesent luptatum zzril delenit augue duis dolore te feugait nulla facilisi. Nam liber tempor cum

11/14 PT ROCKWELL REGULAR
UT WISI ENIM AD MINIM VENIAM, QUIS NOSTRUD EXERCI tation ullamcorper suscipit lobortis nisl ut aliquip ex ea commodo consequat. Duis autem vel eum iriure dolor in hendrerit in vulputate velit esse molestie consequat, vel illum dolore eu feugiat nulla facilisis at vero eros et accumsan et iusto odio dignissim qui blandit

Rockwell Light

abcdefghijklmnopqrstuvwxyz 1234567890
ABCDEFGHIJKLMNOPQRSTUVWXYZ

Rockwell Light Italic

abcdefghijklmnopqrstuvwxyz 1234567890
ABCDEFGHIJKLMNOPQRSTUVWXYZ

Rockwell Italic

abcdefghijklmnopqrstuvwxyz 1234567890
ABCDEFGHIJKLMNOPQRSTUVWXYZ

Rockwell Bold

abcdefghijklmnopqrstuvwxyz 1234567890
ABCDEFGHIJKLMNOPQRSTUVWXYZ

Rockwell Extra Bold

abcdefghijklmnopqrstuvwxyz
1234567890 ABCDEFGHIJKLMNOPQ

Rockwell Regular

abcdefghijklm
nopqrstuvwxyz
ABCDEFGHIJKLM
NOPQRSTUVWXYZ
1234567890 ¼ ½ ¾
[àóüßç](.,:;?!$€£&-*)
{ÀÓÜÇ}

PMN CAECILIA

TYPE DESIGNER: Peter Matthias Noordzij ¶ **FIRST APPEARANCE:** 1991
CLASSIFICATION: Humanist Slab

USE FOR: E-readers and text printed on low-quality paper stock

The first drawings for PMN Caecilia were produced in the 1980s while Peter Matthias Noordzij was a third-year student at the prestigious *Koninklijke Academie van Beeldende Kunsten* (The Royal Academy of Art) in The Hague, Netherlands. It's a landmark typeface as it combined elements of both Humanist and Geometric Slabs, making it the earliest member of the very exclusive Neo-Humanist Slab club. The name of the face combines Peter's initials with his wife Marie-Cécile's name. His drawings grabbed the attention of several foundries at the ATypI conference in London in 1984, and a commercial release by Linotype eventually followed in 1991. It's a fairly simple face to spot as there are few like it – italic styles are cursive, bucking the trend for most other slabs – and its legibility is second to none. This helps explain why it was chosen as one of the default font options on Amazon's Kindle eReader.

KEY FEATURES FOR CLASSIFICATION AND IDENTIFICATION

- Minimal contrast with a large x-height
- Slightly angled stress
- Arches end with a vertical stroke
- Unbracketed serifs with width very close to that of the stems

8/11 PT PMN CAECILIA 55 ROMAN
LOREM IPSUM DOLOR SIT AMET, CONSECTETUER ADIPISCING ELIT, SED DIAM NONUMMY NIBH euismod tincidunt ut laoreet dolore magna aliquam erat volutpat. Ut wisi enim ad minim veniam, quis nostrud exerci tation ullamcorper suscipit lobortis nisl ut aliquip ex ea commodo consequat. Duis autem vel eum iriure dolor in hendrerit in vulputate velit esse molestie consequat, vel illum dolore eu feugiat nulla facilisis at vsero eros et accumsan et iusto odio dignissim qui blandit praesent luptatum zzril delenit augue duis

11/14 PT PMN CAECILIA 55 ROMAN
UT WISI ENIM AD MINIM VENIAM, QUIS NOSTRUD EXERCI tation ullamcorper suscipit lobortis nisl ut aliquip ex ea commodo consequat. Duis autem vel eum iriure dolor in hendrerit in vulputate velit esse molestie consequat, vel illum dolore eu feugiat nulla facilisis at vero eros et accumsan et iusto odio

PNM CAECILIA 45 LIGHT

abcdefghijklmnopqrstuvwxyz 1234567890
ABCDEFGHIJKLMNOPQRSTUVWXYZ

PNM CAECILIA 46 LIGHT ITALIC

abcdefghijklmnopqrstuvwxyz 1234567890
ABCDEFGHIJKLMNOPQRSTUVWXYZ

PNM CAECILIA 56 ITALIC

abcdefghijklmnopqrstuvwxyz 1234567890
ABCDEFGHIJKLMNOPQRSTUVWXYZ

PNM CAECILIA 75 BOLD

abcdefghijklmnopqrstuvwxyz 1234567890
ABCDEFGHIJKLMNOPQRSTUVWXYZ

PNM CAECILIA 85 BOLD

abcdefghijklmnopqrstuvwxyz
1234567890 ABCDEFGHIJKLMNOPQRSTU

PMN CAECILIA 55 ROMAN

abcdefghijklm
nopqrstuvwxyz
ABCDEFGHIJKLM
NOPQRSTUVWXYZ
1234567890 ¼ ½ ¾
[àóüßç](.,:;?!$€£&-*)
{ÀÓÜÇ}

ARCHER

TYPE DESIGNERS: Hoefler & Co. ¶ **FIRST APPEARANCE:** 2008
CLASSIFICATION: Geometric Slab

USE FOR: Brightening up lists and other hierarchical text

Archer isn't your average Geometric Slab and its tremendous popularity holds true to the singular qualities of this typeface. It was commissioned by the publishers of *Martha Stewart Living*, a well known US lifestyle magazine, with the brief going to Hoefler & Co. (then known as Hoefler & Frere-Jones). Most Geometric Slabs look quite steely with an engineered structure, but Hoefler & Co. managed to inject considerable character into the letterforms using generous curves, open bowls and, most effectively, ball terminals on several key characters. In this sense Archer is a kind of hybrid, combining Grotesque and Geometric Slab properties. This combination of established retro alongside contemporary form proved a massive hit with designers when the type family was released commercially in 2008. As one would expect from a Hoefler & Co. face, the character set is extensive, making it a great choice for text that needs a lot of built-in hierarchy.

KEY FEATURES FOR CLASSIFICATION AND IDENTIFICATION

- Minimal contrast with a low x-height
- Vertical stress
- Ball terminals, unusual for a slab serif
- Unbracketed serifs with width equal to that of the stems

8/11 PT ARCHER BOOK
LOREM IPSUM DOLOR SIT AMET, CONSECTETUER ADIPISCING ELIT, SED DIAM NONUMMY NIBH euismod tincidunt ut laoreet dolore magna aliquam erat volutpat. Ut wisi enim ad minim veniam, quis nostrud exerci tation ullamcorper suscipit lobortis nisl ut aliquip ex ea commodo consequat. Duis autem vel eum iriure dolor in hendrerit in vulputate velit esse molestie consequat, vel illum dolore eu feugiat nulla facilisis at vsero eros et accumsan et iusto odio dignissim qui blandit praesent luptatum zzril delenit augue duis dolore te feugait nulla facilisi. Nam liber tempor cum soluta nobis eleifend option congue nihil imperdiet

11/14 PT ARCHER BOOK
UT WISI ENIM AD MINIM VENIAM, QUIS NOSTRUD EXERCI tation ullamcorper suscipit lobortis nisl ut aliquip ex ea commodo consequat. Duis autem vel eum iriure dolor in hendrerit in vulputate velit esse molestie consequat, vel illum dolore eu feugiat nulla facilisis at vero eros et accumsan et iusto odio dignissim qui blandit praesent luptatum zzril

ARCHER HAIRLINE

abcdefghijklmnopqrstuvwxyz 1234567890
ABCDEFGHIJKLMNOPQRSTUVWXYZ

ARCHER EXTRA LIGHT

abcdefghijklmnopqrstuvwxyz 1234567890
ABCDEFGHIJKLMNOPQRSTUVWXYZ

ARCHER BOOK ITALIC

abcdefghijklmnopqrstuvwxyz 1234567890
ABCDEFGHIJKLMNOPQRSTUVWXYZ

ARCHER SEMIBOLD

abcdefghijklmnopqrstuvwxyz 1234567890
ABCDEFGHIJKLMNOPQRSTUVWXYZ

ARCHER BOLD

abcdefghijklmnopqrstuvwxyz 1234567890
ABCDEFGHIJKLMNOPQRSTUVWXYZ

ARCHER BOOK

abcdefghijklm
nopqrstuvwxyz
ABCDEFGHIJKLM
NOPQRSTUVWXYZ
1234567890 ¼ ½ ¾
[àóüßç](.,:;?!$€£&-*)
{ÀÓÜÇ}

Wilhelm Klingspor Schrift

TYPE DESIGNER: Rudolf Koch ¶ **FIRST APPEARANCE:** 1919–1925
CLASSIFICATION: Blackletter/Textura

USE FOR: Graduation certificates and beer labels

Wilhelm Klingspor Schrift (or Wilhelm Klingspor Gotisch) was designed by Rudolf Koch for the Klingspor Type Foundry of Offenbach am Main between 1919 and 1925. It's a member of the general classification Blackletter but is specifically a Textura; Texturas are sometimes also incorrectly referred to as Old English. Harking back to the style of lettering popular in Germany in the mid-fifteenth century (think Gutenberg's Bible), Wilhelm Klingspor Schrift is a beautiful interpretation of the style with just enough elegant decoration, meaning this singular face is surprisingly readable for those of us used to roman letterforms. Koch intentionally pared back the decoration, particularly in the lowercase characters, and created simpler alternative glyphs to increase legibility at smaller point sizes. To understand the differences between Texturas and Frakturs, the other principal sub-classification of a Blackletter, refer to a typeface named Fette Fraktur as a comparison.

KEY FEATURES FOR CLASSIFICATION AND IDENTIFICATION

- High contrast with a large x-height
- Angled stress
- Some glyphs have simplified alternatives
- Thinnest strokes emulate 'pen angle'

8/11 PT WILHELM KLINGSPOR SCHRIFT

LOREM IPSUM DOLOR SIT AMET, CONSECTETUER ADIPISCING ELIT, SED DIAM NONUMMY NIBH EUISMOD tincidunt ut laoreet dolore magna aliquam erat volutpat. Ut wisi enim ad minim veniam, quis nostrud exerci tation ullamcorper suscipit lobortis nisl ut aliquip ex ea commodo consequat. Duis autem vel eum iriure dolor in hendrerit in vulputate velit esse molestie consequat, vel illum dolore eu feugiat nulla facilisis at vero eros et accumsan et iusto odio dignissim qui blandit praesent luptatum zzril delenit augue duis dolore te feugait nulla facilisi. Nam liber tempor cum soluta nobis eleifend option congue nihil imperdiet doming id quod mazim placerat facer possim assum. Typi non habent claritatem insitam; est usus legentis in iis qui facit eorum claritatem. Investigationes demonstraverunt lectores legere me lius quod ii legunt saepius. Claritas est etiam

11/14 PT WILHELM KLINGSPOR SCHRIFT

UT WISI ENIM AD MINIM VENIAM, QUIS NOSTRUD EXERCI TATION ullamcorper suscipit lobortis nisl ut aliquip ex ea commodo consequat. Duis autem vel eum iriure dolor in hendrerit in vulputate velit esse molestie consequat, vel illum dolore eu feugiat nulla facilisis at vero eros et accumsan et iusto odio dignissim qui blandit praesent luptatum zzril delenit augue duis dolore te feugait nulla facilisi. Nam liber tempor cum soluta nobis eleifend option congue nihil imperdiet doming id quod mazim placerat

abcdefghijklm

nopqrstuvwxyz

ABCDEFGHI

JKLMNOPQ

RSTUVWXYZ

1234567890

[àöüßç]

(.,;?!&&*)

{ÀÓÙÇ}

Bickham Script

TYPE DESIGNER: Richard Lipton ¶ **FIRST APPEARANCE:** 1997
CLASSIFICATION: Formal Script

USE FOR: Wedding invitations or facsimiles of formal handwriting

Despite what I suggest above, Formal Script typefaces are not designed exclusively for use in wedding invitations, although they do undeniably work in that context. Setting text in any script face represented perhaps the biggest challenge for typographers before the advent of digital fonts and OpenType. Achieving an even flow between consecutive characters involved a great deal of work and it was often easier to simply commission hand-lettered artwork. Bickham Script was designed by the calligrapher Richard Lipton and released by Adobe in 1997 as one of the earliest fonts to take advantage of alternative glyph and ligature substitution, with its built-in ability to substitute different pairings of glyphs, dynamically selecting contextual variations as words are formed. Bickham Script remains the benchmark by which other digital Formal Scripts are compared and contains over 1,700 individual glyphs. Using this typeface to its best ability requires practice but the results are well worth it.

KEY FEATURES FOR CLASSIFICATION AND IDENTIFICATION

- High contrast with a very low x-height
- Angled stress based on lowercase 'o'
- Many alternative glyphs
- Looped crossbar on the 'A'

18PT BICKHAM SCRIPT REGULAR

36PT BICKHAM SCRIPT REGULAR

72PT BICKHAM SCRIPT REGULAR

Bickham Script Semibold

abcdefghijklmnopqrstuvwxyz

1234567890 ABCDEFGHIJK

LMNOPQRSTUVWXYZ

Bickham Script Bold

abcdefghijklmnopqrstuvwxyz

1234567890 ABCDEFGHIJK

LMNOPQRSTUVWXYZ

Bickham Script Regular

abcdefghhhhijklm

nopqrstuvwxyz

ABCDEFGHIJKLM

NOPQRSTUVWXYZ

1234567890 ¼ ½ ¾

[àóüßç/](.,:;?!$€£&-*)

{ÀÓÜÇ}

Suomi Hand Script

Type designer: Tomi Haaparanta ¶ **First appearance:** 2008
Classification: Casual Script

Use for: Realistic handwritten annotations

There have been many attempts over the years to create a font that looks like real 'everyday' handwriting. I'm talking about the kind of writing you find in hastily scrawled shopping lists or on the sticky note stuck to the refrigerator door. Most of these attempts fail to deliver a truly convincing solution because they're too regular; either the repeat characters are all exactly the same, consecutive letters form unnatural links, or alignment is simply too neat. However, Suomi Hand Script manages to succeed where others have failed because it utilises hundreds of ligatures and dozens of alternative glyphs to create a very convincing facsimile of real handwriting. Tomi Haaparanta of the Finnish digital foundry Suomi released this very useful typeface in 2008 and, to the best of my knowledge, there are no newer faces that do a better job than this.

Key Features for Classification and Identification

- Minimum contrast with an irregular x-height
- Variable angled stress
- Baseline shifts for alternative glyph pairs
- Strokes heaviest at start of 'pen stroke'

8/11 PT SUOMI HAND SCRIPT

LOREM IPSUM DOLOR SIT AMET, CONSECTETUER ADIPISCING ELIT, SED DIAM NONUMMY NIBH EUISMOD TINCIDUNT UT LAOREET DOLORE MAGNA ALIQUAM ERAT VOLUTPAT. UT WISI ENIM AD minim veniam, quis nostrud exerci tation ullamcorper suscipit lobortis nisl ut aliquip ex ea commodo consequat. Duis autem vel eum iriure dolor in hendrerit in vulputate velit esse molestie consequat, vel illum dolore eu feugiat nulla facilisis at vero eros et accumsan et iusto odio dignissim qui blandit praesent luptatum zzril delenit augue duis dolore te feugait nulla facilisi. Nam liber tempor cum soluta nobis eleifend option congue nihil imperdiet doming id quod mazim placerat facer possim assum. Typi non habent claritatem insitam; est usus legentis in iis qui facit eorum claritatem. Investigationes demonstraverunt lectores legere me lius quod ii legunt saepius. Claritas est etiam processus dynamicus, qui sequitur mutationem consuetudium lectorum. Mirum est notare quam littera gothica, quam nunc putamus parum claram, anteposuerit litterarum formas

11/14 PT SUOMI HAND SCRIPT

UT WISI ENIM AD MINIM VENIAM, QUIS NOSTRUD EXERCI TATION ULLAMCORPER SUSCIPIT LOBORTIS NISL UT ALIQUIP EX EA COMMODO consequat. Duis autem vel eum iriure dolor in hendrerit in vulputate velit esse molestie consequat, vel illum dolore eu feugiat nulla facilisis at vero eros et accumsan et iusto odio dignissim qui blandit praesent luptatum zzril delenit augue duis dolore te feugait nulla facilisi. Nam liber tempor cum soluta nobis eleifend option congue nihil imperdiet doming id quod mazim placerat facer possim assum. Typi non habent claritatem insitam; est usus legentis in iis qui facit eorum claritatem.

abcdefghijklm

nopqrstuvwxyz

ABCDEFGHIJ

KLMNOPQRST

UVWXYZ

1234567890 ¼ ½ ¾

[àóüßç](.,:;?!$€£&-*)

{ÀÓÜÇ}

The Carpenter

TYPE DESIGNER: Emil Karl Bertell ¶ **FIRST APPEARANCE:** 2014
CLASSIFICATION: Casual Script

USE FOR: Creating flamboyant hand-lettered headlines

Like Bickham Script (see page 140), The Carpenter takes full advantage of the automatic glyph and ligature substitution functionality built into the OpenType format. Designed by Emil Karl Bertell at Fenotype, a digital foundry which specializes in script and display faces, The Carpenter appeared in 2014. It's loosely based on an earlier Bertell typeface named Mercury Script, which was in turn based on a sample of hand lettering spotted in a vintage lingerie advertisement. Casual Scripts like The Carpenter share a close relationship with the retro lettering of many a mid-century advertisement, typically of North American origin. Glyph substitution can be carried out manually if one wishes, or can be activated using the OpenType settings of software such as Adobe's InDesign; just select Swash, Contextual Alternates, Stylistic Sets and so on to see the results unfold. Be sure to use the Metrics setting for character spacing as Optical spacing won't work with a connected script face like this.

144

KEY FEATURES FOR CLASSIFICATION AND IDENTIFICATION

- High contrast with a low x-height
- Angled stress
- Many alternative glyphs (see right)
- All caps have alternative swash glyphs

18PT THE CARPENTER REGULAR

Ragtorpestry

36PT THE CARPENTER REGULAR

Ragtorpestry

72PT THE CARPENTER REGULAR

The Carpenter Bold

abcdefghijklmnopqrstuvwxyz 1234567890

ABCDEFGHIJKLM

OPQRSTUVWXYZ

The Carpenter Black

abcdefghijklmnopqrstuvwxyz

1234567890

ABCDEFGHIJKLM

OPQRSTUVWXYZ

The Carpenter Regular

abbbbcdefghijklm

nopqrstuvwxyz

ABCDEFGHIJKLM

NOPQRSTUVWXYZ

1234567890 ¼ ½ ¾

[àöüßç](.,:;?!$€£&-*)

{ ÀÖÜÇ }

AKZIDENZ-GROTESK

TYPE DESIGNERS: H. Berthold AG staff ¶ FIRST APPEARANCE: 1898
CLASSIFICATION: Grotesque Sans

USE FOR: Workaday headlines and plain, unassuming text

Akzidenz-Grotesk is arguably one of the most influential typefaces still in regular use. Unusually for such a popular face, it has no single accredited designer because it was created jointly by the staff of Berthold Type Foundry in Berlin in the late 1890s as their 'jobbing' typeface, one that could be used as a kind of default for just about anything. Intended for display use, subsequent updates to the original single weight were carried out in piecemeal fashion until a 1950s effort by the typographer Günter Gerhard Lange (a longtime art director at Berthold) pulled the unruly type family into shape and improved its capabilities as a general text face. This was, of course, around the same time as the growth of the International Typographic Style or the Swiss Style, and Akzidenz-Grotesk was a major influence on the design of Neue Haas Grotesk, which subsequently became Helvetica. It's not easy to tell the two faces apart, but the straight leg of the 'R' of Akzidenz-Grotesk provides a giveaway clue.

KEY FEATURES FOR CLASSIFICATION AND IDENTIFICATION

- Minimal contrast with a moderate x-height
- Vertical stress
- Terminals are angled
- Tails are omitted from heavier weights

8/11 PT BERTHOLD AKZIDENZ-GROTESK

LOREM IPSUM DOLOR SIT AMET, CONSECTETUER ADIPISCING ELIT, SED DIAM NONUMMY NIBH euismod tincidunt ut laoreet dolore magna aliquam erat volutpat. Ut wisi enim ad minim veniam, quis nostrud exerci tation ullamcorper suscipit lobortis nisl ut aliquip ex ea commodo consequat. Duis autem vel eum iriure dolor in hendrerit in vulputate velit esse molestie consequat, vel illum dolore eu feugiat nulla facilisis at vsero eros et accumsan et iusto odio dignissim qui blandit praesent luptatum zzril delenit augue duis dolore te feugait nulla facilisi. Nam liber tempor cum soluta nobis eleifend option congue nihil imperdiet

11/14 PT BERTHOLD AKZIDENZ-GROTESK

UT WISI ENIM AD MINIM VENIAM, QUIS NOSTRUD EXERCI tation ullamcorper suscipit lobortis nisl ut aliquip ex ea commodo consequat. Duis autem vel eum iriure dolor in hendrerit in vulputate velit esse molestie consequat, vel illum dolore eu feugiat nulla facilisis at vero eros et accumsan et iusto odio dignissim qui blandit praesent luptatum zzril delenit augue

Akzidenz-Grotesk Light

abcdefghijklmnopqrstuvwxyz 1234567890
ABCDEFGHIJKLMNOPQRSTUVWXYZ

Akzidenz-Grotesk Italic

abcdefghijklmnopqrstuvwxyz 1234567890
ABCDEFGHIJKLMNOPQRSTUVWXYZ

Akzidenz-Grotesk Medium

abcdefghijklmnopqrstuvwxyz 1234567890
ABCDEFGHIJKLMNOPQRSTUVWXYZ

Akzidenz-Grotesk Bold

abcdefghijklmnopqrstuvwxyz 1234567890
ABCDEFGHIJKLMNOPQRSTUVWXYZ

Akzidenz-Grotesk Super

abcdefghijklmnopqrstuvwxyz
1234567890 ABCDEFGHIJKLMNOPQR

Berthold Akzidenz-Grotesk

abcdefghijklm
nopqrstuvwxyz
ABCDEFGHIJKLM
NOPQRSTUVWXYZ
1234567890 ¼ ½ ¾
[àóüßç](.,:;?!$€£&-*)
{ÀÓÜÇ}

FRANKLIN GOTHIC

TYPE DESIGNER: Morris Fuller Benton ¶ **FIRST APPEARANCE:** 1902–1912
CLASSIFICATION: Gothic Sans

USE FOR: Punchy headlines paired with News Gothic text setting

What Akzidenz-Grotesk is to Europe, Franklin Gothic is to the United States. Gothic was used in the US as an equivalent term to the German Grotesk (or the British Grotesque) to describe early sans serif typefaces in general, and it's likely that the typeface designer Morris Fuller Benton was influenced by Akzidenz-Grotesk when he began designing Franklin Gothic in 1902. Designed to be a hard-working sans serif for everyday use (just like Akzidenz-Grotesk), Franklin Gothic was only available in a single weight for several years following its initial release, but that didn't diminish its popularity. As a consequence a limited number of additional widths and an italic were designed by Benton during the following ten years, but it wasn't until 1979 that a more complete family was created by Victor Caruso for the International Typeface Corporation. This expanded range of weights, with their oblique roman italic styles, is the one we're used to seeing and using today.

KEY FEATURES FOR CLASSIFICATION AND IDENTIFICATION
- Minimal contrast with a large x-height
- Vertical stress
- Terminals are angled
- Tail of 'a' kicks out slightly

8/11 PT ITC FRANKLIN GOTHIC BOOK

LOREM IPSUM DOLOR SIT AMET, CONSECTETUER ADIPISCING ELIT, SED DIAM NONUMMY NIBH EUISMOD tincidunt ut laoreet dolore magna aliquam erat volutpat. Ut wisi enim ad minim veniam, quis nostrud exerci tation ullamcorper suscipit lobortis nisl ut aliquip ex ea commodo consequat. Duis autem vel eum iriure dolor in hendrerit in vulputate velit esse molestie consequat, vel illum dolore eu feugiat nulla facilisis at vsero eros et accumsan et iusto odio dignissim qui blandit praesent luptatum zzril delenit augue duis dolore te feugait nulla facilisi. Nam liber tempor cum soluta nobis eleifend option congue nihil

11/14 PT ITC FRANKLIN GOTHIC BOOK

UT WISI ENIM AD MINIM VENIAM, QUIS NOSTRUD EXERCI TATION ullamcorper suscipit lobortis nisl ut aliquip ex ea commodo consequat. Duis autem vel eum iriure dolor in hendrerit in vulputate velit esse molestie consequat, vel illum dolore eu feugiat nulla facilisis at vero eros et accumsan et iusto odio dignissim qui blandit praesent luptatum zzril

ITC FRANKLIN GOTHIC BOOK ITALIC

abcdefghijklmnopqrstuvwxyz 1234567890
ABCDEFGHIJKLMNOPQRSTUVWXYZ

ITC FRANKLIN GOTHIC MEDIUM

abcdefghijklmnopqrstuvwxyz 1234567890
ABCDEFGHIJKLMNOPQRSTUVWXYZ

ITC FRANKLIN GOTHIC DEMI

abcdefghijklmnopqrstuvwxyz 1234567890
ABCDEFGHIJKLMNOPQRSTUVWXYZ

ITC FRANKLIN GOTHIC DEMI ITALIC

abcdefghijklmnopqrstuvwxyz 1234567890
ABCDEFGHIJKLMNOPQRSTUVWXYZ

ITC FRANKLIN GOTHIC HEAVY

abcdefghijklmnopqrstuvwxyz 1234567890
ABCDEFGHIJKLMNOPQRSTUVWXYZ

ITC FRANKLIN GOTHIC BOOK

abcdefghijklm
nopqrstuvwxyz
ABCDEFGHIJKLM
NOPQRSTUVWXYZ
1234567890 ¼½¾
[àóüßç](.,:;?!$€£&-*)
{ÀÓÜÇ}

NEWS GOTHIC

TYPE DESIGNER: Morris Fuller Benton ¶ **FIRST APPEARANCE:** 1908
CLASSIFICATION: Gothic Sans

USE FOR: Space-saving text of an everyday nature

News Gothic is in a way a sibling to Franklin Gothic (see page 148); the original weights of both typefaces were designed by Morris Fuller Benton within a six-year period of one another with a similar end use in mind. News Gothic was aimed squarely at the newspaper publishing industry – the clue is there in the name – and once again Benton designed only three widths without italic styles. Essentially a lighter version of Franklin Gothic, printers could use News Gothic for running text and Franklin Gothic for headlines, and it became the most popular 'jobbing' sans serif text face in the US for almost thirty years. Its narrower width is the best way to distinguish it from Franklin Gothic, and it shouldn't be confused with Trade Gothic, which is simply Linotype's 1948 version of News Gothic under a different name. For a contemporary take on News Gothic, look no further than the extensive Benton Sans family designed by Tobias Frere-Jones and Cyrus Highsmith for Font Bureau.

KEY FEATURES FOR CLASSIFICATION AND IDENTIFICATION
- Minimal contrast with a large x-height
- Vertical stress
- The bowl of the 'a' shelves very steeply
- Curved tail of the 'Q' is central and extends vertically downwards

8/11 PT NEWS GOTHIC ROMAN

LOREM IPSUM DOLOR SIT AMET, CONSECTETUER ADIPISCING ELIT, SED DIAM NONUMMY NIBH EUISMOD tincidunt ut laoreet dolore magna aliquam erat volutpat. Ut wisi enim ad minim veniam, quis nostrud exerci tation ullamcorper suscipit lobortis nisl ut aliquip ex ea commodo consequat. Duis autem vel eum iriure dolor in hendrerit in vulputate velit esse molestie consequat, vel illum dolore eu feugiat nulla facilisis at vsero eros et accumsan et iusto odio dignissim qui blandit praesent luptatum zzril delenit augue duis dolore te feugait nulla facilisi. Nam liber tempor cum soluta nobis eleifend option congue nihil imperdiet doming id quod mazim placerat facer possim assum. Typi non

11/14 PT NEWS GOTHIC ROMAN

UT WISI ENIM AD MINIM VENIAM, QUIS NOSTRUD EXERCI TATION ULLAMCORPER suscipit lobortis nisl ut aliquip ex ea commodo consequat. Duis autem vel eum iriure dolor in hendrerit in vulputate velit esse molestie consequat, vel illum dolore eu feugiat nulla facilisis at vero eros et accumsan et iusto odio dignissim qui blandit praesent luptatum zzril delenit augue duis dolore te feugait nulla facilisi. Nam liber tempor

News Gothic Light
abcdefghijklmnopqrstuvwxyz 1234567890
ABCDEFGHIJKLMNOPQRSTUVWXYZ

News Gothic Italic
abcdefghijklmnopqrstuvwxyz 1234567890
ABCDEFGHIJKLMNOPQRSTUVWXYZ

News Gothic Medium
abcdefghijklmnopqrstuvwxyz 1234567890
ABCDEFGHIJKLMNOPQRSTUVWXYZ

News Gothic Bold
abcdefghijklmnopqrstuvwxyz 1234567890
ABCDEFGHIJKLMNOPQRSTUVWXYZ

News Gothic Black
abcdefghijklmnopqrstuvwxyz 1234567890
ABCDEFGHIJKLMNOPQRSTUVWXYZ

News Gothic Roman
abcdefghijklm
nopqrstuvwxyz
ABCDEFGHIJKLM
NOPQRSTUVWXYZ
1234567890 ¼ ½ ¾
[àóüßç](.,:;?!$€£&-*)
{ÀÓÜÇ}

FUTURA

Type designer: Paul Renner ¶ **First appearance:** 1927–1930
Classification: Geometric Sans

Use for: Futuristic topics observed from a retro perspective

Despite it being almost ninety years old, Paul Renner's 1927 Geometric Sans Futura has never quite gone out of fashion, and it's still frequently used to express futuristic typographic themes. The face has strong associations with the Bauhaus, despite Renner having no formal association with the school; this is probably due to the timing of Futura's release and because Renner shared the same views expressed by Bauhaus tutors and students. He also detested the association of traditional Blackletter faces with the Nazis and openly criticized the regime – to his eventual cost. Futura is an easy face to spot with its strict geometry – the single-storey lowercase 'a' and the uppercase 'M', with its splayed stems, are key identifiers – but this same geometry creates issues of legibility. Renner did attempt to address this by adjusting the proportions of some characters, but a cautionary approach should be taken when considering its use for running text. At larger point sizes the legibility issues are far less problematic.

Key Features for Classification and Identification

- Minimal contrast with a fairly low x-height
- Vertical stress
- Round dots
- Pointed vertices descend below baseline

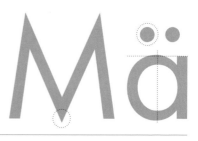

8/11 pt Futura ND Book

LOREM IPSUM DOLOR SIT AMET, CONSECTETUER ADIPISCING ELIT, SED DIAM NONUMMY NIBH euismod tincidunt ut laoreet dolore magna aliquam erat volutpat. Ut wisi enim ad minim veniam, quis nostrud exerci tation ullamcorper suscipit lobortis nisl ut aliquip ex ea commodo consequat. Duis autem vel eum iriure dolor in hendrerit in vulputate velit esse molestie consequat, vel illum dolore eu feugiat nulla facilisis at vsero eros et accumsan et iusto odio dignissim qui blandit praesent luptatum zzril delenit augue duis dolore te feugait nulla facilisi. Nam liber tempor cum soluta nobis eleifend option congue nihil

11/14 pt Futura ND Book

UT WISI ENIM AD MINIM VENIAM, QUIS NOSTRUD EXERCI TATION ullamcorper suscipit lobortis nisl ut aliquip ex ea commodo consequat. Duis autem vel eum iriure dolor in hendrerit in vulputate velit esse molestie consequat, vel illum dolore eu feugiat nulla facilisis at vero eros et accumsan et iusto odio dignissim qui blandit praesent luptatum zzril

Futura ND Light

abcdefghijklmnopqrstuvwxyz 1234567890
ABCDEFGHIJKLMNOPQRSTUVWXYZ

Futura ND Book Oblique

abcdefghijklmnopqrstuvwxyz 1234567890
ABCDEFGHIJKLMNOPQRSTUVWXYZ

Futura ND Medium

abcdefghijklmnopqrstuvwxyz 1234567890
ABCDEFGHIJKLMNOPQRSTUVWXYZ

Futura ND Demibold

abcdefghijklmnopqrstuvwxyz
1234567890 ABCDEFGHIJKLMNOPQRST

Futura ND Bold

abcdefghijklmnopqrstuvwxyz
1234567890 ABCDEFGHIJKLMNOPQR

Futura ND Book

abcdefghijklm
nopqrstuvwxyz
ABCDEFGHIJKLM
NOPQRSTUVWXYZ
1234567890 ¼ ½ ¾
[àóüßç](.,:;?!$€£&-*)
{ÀÓÜÇ}

GILL SANS

TYPE DESIGNER: Eric Gill ¶ **FIRST APPEARANCE:** 1928–1930
CLASSIFICATION: Humanist Sans

USE FOR: Anything that requires a quintessentially British feel

Of all the sans serif typefaces, Gill Sans (like its creator) is a bit of a strange one. In keeping with the typographic sensibilities of its time it has features you'd expect to find in a Geometric Sans, but characters like the double-storey 'a' and the 'g' with its binocular form defy this classification. It is in fact a Humanist Sans; the variable stroke contrast combined with Gill's stone carver aesthetic make it so. In actual fact, the letterforms are based on hand lettering painted on a shopfront in Bristol by Gill and spotted by Monotype's Stanley Morison. Despite its display face origins, Gill Sans' Humanist qualities mean it's capable of producing highly legible text which is rich in character, but don't assume it'll give you an easy time. Character spacing can be tricky so expect some manual kerning requirements here and there. In 2015, Monotype released Gill Sans Nova, an augmented family of forty-three separate styles with enhanced glyph sets.

KEY FEATURES FOR CLASSIFICATION AND IDENTIFICATION

- Variable contrast with a moderate x-height
- Vertical stress
- Leg of the 'R' extends far beyond body
- The 't' features a triangular bracket

8/11 PT GILL SANS BOOK

LOREM IPSUM DOLOR SIT AMET, CONSECTETUER ADIPISCING ELIT, SED DIAM NONUMMY NIBH EUISMOD tincidunt ut laoreet dolore magna aliquam erat volutpat. Ut wisi enim ad minim veniam, quis nostrud exerci tation ullamcorper suscipit lobortis nisl ut aliquip ex ea commodo consequat. Duis autem vel eum iriure dolor in hendrerit in vulputate velit esse molestie consequat, vel illum dolore eu feugiat nulla facilisis at vsero eros et accumsan et iusto odio dignissim qui blandit praesent luptatum zzril delenit augue duis dolore te feugait nulla facilisi. Nam liber tempor cum soluta nobis eleifend option congue nihil imperdiet doming id quod mazim placerat facer

11/14 PT GILL SANS BOOK

UT WISI ENIM AD MINIM VENIAM, QUIS NOSTRUD EXERCI TATION ullamcorper suscipit lobortis nisl ut aliquip ex ea commodo consequat. Duis autem vel eum iriure dolor in hendrerit in vulputate velit esse molestie consequat, vel illum dolore eu feugiat nulla facilisis at vero eros et accumsan et iusto odio dignissim qui blandit praesent luptatum zzril delenit augue duis dolore te feugait nulla

GILL SANS LIGHT
abcdefghijklmnopqrstuvwxyz 1234567890
ABCDEFGHIJKLMNOPQRSTUVWXYZ

GILL SANS BOOK ITALIC
abcdefghijklmnopqrstuvwxyz 1234567890
ABCDEFGHIJKLMNOPQRSTUVWXYZ

GILL SANS MEDIUM
abcdefghijklmnopqrstuvwxyz 1234567890
ABCDEFGHIJKLMNOPQRSTUVWXYZ

GILL SANS BOLD
abcdefghijklmnopqrstuvwxyz 1234567890
ABCDEFGHIJKLMNOPQRSTUVWXYZ

GILL SANS HEAVY
abcdefghijklmnopqrstuvwxyz
1234567890 ABCDEFGHIJKLMNOPQRS

GILL SANS BOOK
abcdefghijklm
nopqrstuvwxyz
ABCDEFGHIJKLM
NOPQRSTUVWXYZ
1234567890 ¼ ½ ¾
[àóüßç](.,:;?!$€£&-*)
{ÀÓÜÇ}

DIN

TYPE DESIGNERS: German Institute for Standardization
FIRST APPEARANCE: 1931 ¶ **CLASSIFICATION:** Geometric Sans

USE FOR: Typography requiring Teutonic precision; road signs

DIN 1451, the first incarnation of this very German Geometric Sans, was developed at the *Deutsches Institut für Normung*, which translates as the German Institute for Standardization and gives the typeface its abbreviated name. It was designed by committee and originally intended for use on public signage and other official printed matter. The proportions of each character were designed to conform to a grid so non-professional typographers could letter-space it correctly, and there was initially just one weight. There are many more options available now thanks to various foundries' development of the original letterforms; for example DIN 30640 was added by Linotype around 1970, FF DIN is a ten-weight family that includes condensed weights and italic styles, and the even larger DIN Next family has fourteen weights. Look for the flat-sided round characters and square dots when identifying this typeface.

KEY FEATURES FOR CLASSIFICATION AND IDENTIFICATION

- Minimal contrast with a large x-height
- Vertical stress
- The dots are square
- The bowl of the 'a' is horizontal

8/11 PT DIN 1451 MITTELSCHRIFT

LOREM IPSUM DOLOR SIT AMET,
CONSECTETUER ADIPISCING ELIT, SED
DIAM NONUMMY NIBH EUISMOD
tincidunt ut laoreet dolore magna
aliquam erat volutpat. Ut wisi enim ad
minim veniam, quis nostrud exerci tation
ullamcorper suscipit lobortis nisl ut
aliquip ex ea commodo consequat. Duis
autem vel eum iriure dolor in hendrerit in
vulputate velit esse molestie consequat,
vel illum dolore eu feugiat nulla facilisis
at vsero eros et accumsan et iusto odio
dignissim qui blandit praesent luptatum
zzril delenit augue duis dolore te feugait
nulla facilisi. Nam liber tempor cum
soluta nobis eleifend option congue nihil
imperdiet doming id quod mazim

11/14 PT DIN 1451 MITTELSCHRIFT

UT WISI ENIM AD
MINIM VENIAM, QUIS
NOSTRUD EXERCI TATION
ullamcorper suscipit lobortis
nisl ut aliquip ex ea commodo
consequat. Duis autem vel
eum iriure dolor in hendrerit
in vulputate velit esse
molestie consequat, vel illum
dolore eu feugiat nulla
facilisis at vero eros et
accumsan et iusto odio
dignissim qui blandit praesent
luptatum zzril delenit augue

DIN 1451 Engschrift

abcdefghijklmnopqrstuvwxyz 1234567890
ABCDEFGHIJKLMNOPQRSTUVWXYZ

DIN 30640 Neuzeit Grotesk Light

abcdefghijklmnopqrstuvwxyz 1234567890
ABCDEFGHIJKLMNOPQRSTUVWXYZ

DIN 30640 Neuzeit Grotesk Bold Condensed

abcdefghijklmnopqrstuvwxyz 1234567890
ABCDEFGHIJKLMNOPQRSTUVWXYZ

DIN 1451 Mittelschrift

abcdefghijklm
nopqrstuvwxyz
ABCDEFGHIJKLM
NOPQRSTUVWXYZ
1234567890 ¼ ½ ¾
[àóüßç](.,:;?!$€£&-*)
{ÀÓÜÇ}

FOLIO

Type designers: Konrad F. Bauer and Walter Baum
First appearance: 1957-1962 ¶ **Classification:** Neo-Grotesque Sans

Use for: An alternative to the ever-present and overused Helvetica

Folio was designed by a two-man team, Konrad F. Bauer and Walter Baum, at the Bauer Type Foundry in Frankfurt. Like certain other better-known typefaces released around the same time which went on to represent the International Typographic Style, Folio was influenced significantly by the letterforms of Akzidenz-Grotesk. In fact it's somewhat closer in style to Akzidenz-Grotesk than either Univers or Helvetica because it retains a more moderate x-height. The lack of any italic styles and a smaller range of weights may have contributed to the fact that Folio was not as commercially successful as its Neo-Grotesque colleagues in Europe, but it did a lot better in the United States, where it was popular with newspaper publishers throughout the 1950s and 1960s. It remains a useful, slightly less 'neo' substitute for Helvetica, as long as italics aren't required.

Key Features for Classification and Identification

- Moderate contrast and x-height
- Vertical stress
- Bowl of 'a' is relatively complex
- Curved tail of the 'Q' is central and extends vertically downwards

8/11 pt Folio Light

LOREM IPSUM DOLOR SIT AMET, CONSECTETUER ADIPISCING ELIT, SED DIAM NONUMMY NIBH euismod tincidunt ut laoreet dolore magna aliquam erat volutpat. Ut wisi enim ad minim veniam, quis nostrud exerci tation ullamcorper suscipit lobortis nisl ut aliquip ex ea commodo consequat. Duis autem vel eum iriure dolor in hendrerit in vulputate velit esse molestie consequat, vel illum dolore eu feugiat nulla facilisis at vsero eros et accumsan et iusto odio dignissim qui blandit praesent luptatum zzril delenit augue duis dolore te feugait nulla facilisi. Nam liber tempor cum soluta nobis eleifend option congue nihil imperdiet

11/14 pt Folio Light

UT WISI ENIM AD MINIM VENIAM, QUIS NOSTRUD EXERCI tation ullamcorper suscipit lobortis nisl ut aliquip ex ea commodo consequat. Duis autem vel eum iriure dolor in hendrerit in vulputate velit esse molestie consequat, vel illum dolore eu feugiat nulla facilisis at vero eros et accumsan et iusto odio dignissim qui blandit praesent luptatum zzril

Folio Medium

abcdefghijklmnopqrstuvwxyz 1234567890
ABCDEFGHIJKLMNOPQRSTUVWXYZ

Folio Bold

abcdefghijklmnopqrstuvwxyz
1234567890
ABCDEFGHIJKLMNOPQRSTUVWXYZ

Folio Extra Bold

abcdefghijklmnopqrstuvwxyz
1234567890
ABCDEFGHIJKLMNOPQRSTUVWXYZ

Folio Bold Condensed

abcdefghijklmnopqrstuvwxyz 1234567890
ABCDEFGHIJKLMNOPQRSTUVWXYZ

Folio Light

abcdefghijklm
nopqrstuvwxyz
ABCDEFGHIJKLM
NOPQRSTUVWXYZ
1234567890 ¼ ½ ¾
[àóüßç](.,:;?!$€£&-*)
{ÀÓÜÇ}

UNIVERS

TYPE DESIGNER: Adrian Frutiger ¶ FIRST APPEARANCE: 1957
CLASSIFICATION: Neo-Grotesque Sans

USE FOR: Clear communication with a sense of typographic anonymity

In the early 1950s, the French type foundry Deberny & Peignot identified the need for a fresh sans serif typeface that would work well with the emerging photocomposition technology. To meet the brief, designer Adrian Frutiger persuaded foundry director Charles Peignot that a new Geometric Sans wasn't the answer (Peignot wanted something to compete directly with Futura) and returned to experimental work he'd begun while still a student in Zurich. The result was the immensely successful Univers, a highly legible Neo-Grotesque Sans equally at home with text and display setting. Frutiger's unusual naming system utilising numbered weights and styles was the first of its kind, and the original family contained a total of twenty-one variants ranging from 39 Thin Ultra Condensed to 83 Extra Bold Expanded. The first digit indicates weight, the second indicates width plus style (roman or italic). The remastered Univers Next family with over sixty weights and styles was released by Linotype in 2010.

KEY FEATURES FOR CLASSIFICATION AND IDENTIFICATION

- Low contrast with a moderate x-height
- Vertical stress
- Horizontal tail of 'Q' flicks upwards to align with the baseline
- Bowl of the 'a' is horizontal

8/11 PT UNIVERS 55 ROMAN

LOREM IPSUM DOLOR SIT AMET, CONSECTETUER ADIPISCING ELIT, SED DIAM NONUMMY NIBH euismod tincidunt ut laoreet dolore magna aliquam erat volutpat. Ut wisi enim ad minim veniam, quis nostrud exerci tation ullamcorper suscipit lobortis nisl ut aliquip ex ea commodo consequat. Duis autem vel eum iriure dolor in hendrerit in vulputate velit esse molestie consequat, vel illum dolore eu feugiat nulla facilisis at vsero eros et accumsan et iusto odio dignissim qui blandit praesent luptatum zzril delenit augue duis dolore te feugait nulla facilisi. Nam liber tempor cum

11/14 PT UNIVERS 55 ROMAN

UT WISI ENIM AD MINIM VENIAM, QUIS NOSTRUD EXERCITATION ullamcorper suscipit lobortis nisl ut aliquip ex ea commodo consequat. Duis autem vel eum iriure dolor in hendrerit in vulputate velit esse molestie consequat, vel illum dolore eu feugiat nulla facilisis at vero eros et accumsan et iusto odio dignissim qui blandit

UNIVERS 45 LIGHT

abcdefghijklmnopqrstuvwxyz 1234567890
ABCDEFGHIJKLMNOPQRSTUVWXYZ

UNIVERS 55 OBLIQUE

abcdefghijklmnopqrstuvwxyz 1234567890
ABCDEFGHIJKLMNOPQRSTUVWXYZ

UNIVERS 65 BOLD

abcdefghijklmnopqrstuvwxyz 1234567890
ABCDEFGHIJKLMNOPQRSTUVWXYZ

UNIVERS 75 BLACK

abcdefghijklmnopqrstuvwxyz
1234567890 ABCDEFGHIJKLMNOPQR

UNIVERS 85 EXTRA BLACK

abcdefghijklmnopqrstuvwxyz
1234567890 ABCDEFGHIJKLMNOPQ

UNIVERS 55 ROMAN

abcdefghijklm
nopqrstuvwxyz
ABCDEFGHIJKLM
NOPQRSTUVWXYZ
1234567890 ¼ ½ ¾
[àóüßç](.,:;?!$€£&-*)
{ÀÓÜÇ}

HELVETICA

TYPE DESIGNER: Max Miedinger and Eduard Hoffmann
FIRST APPEARANCE: 1957 ¶ **CLASSIFICATION:** Neo-Grotesque Sans

USE FOR: Clean exhibition displays, straightforward logos

There's little to be said about Helvetica that hasn't already been said – it's the world's best-known typeface and (rather like Times New Roman) non-designers often refer to any sans serifs as 'Helvetica fonts'. It's less well known that the face began life as Neue Haas Grotesk, a 1957 design by Max Miedinger and Eduard Hoffmann for the Haas Type Foundry in Münchenstein, Switzerland. They wanted to create a more refined version of Akzidenz-Grotesk in response to the continued interest in the International Typographic Style or Swiss Style, thus creating one of the first Neo-Grotesque faces. It wasn't until the larger Stempel foundry became involved in manufacturing Neue Haas Grotesk matrices for Linotype in 1961 that, for marketing purposes, the name was changed to Helvetica, the Latin word for 'Swiss'. Neue Helvetica is a 1983 version redrawn by Stempel to harmonize some of the more disparate design elements that had crept into the typeface family during the intermediate years.

KEY FEATURES FOR CLASSIFICATION AND IDENTIFICATION

- Low contrast with moderate x-height
- Vertical stress
- Very small, closed apertures
- Leg of 'R' features a gentle curve

8/11 PT NEUE HELVETICA 55 ROMAN

LOREM IPSUM DOLOR SIT AMET, CONSECTETUER ADIPISCING ELIT, SED DIAM NONUMMY NIBH euismod tincidunt ut laoreet dolore magna aliquam erat volutpat. Ut wisi enim ad minim veniam, quis nostrud exerci tation ullamcorper suscipit lobortis nisl ut aliquip ex ea commodo consequat. Duis autem vel eum iriure dolor in hendrerit in vulputate velit esse molestie consequat, vel illum dolore eu feugiat nulla facilisis at vsero eros et accumsan et iusto odio dignissim qui blandit praesent luptatum zzril delenit augue duis dolore te feugait nulla facilisi. Nam liber tempor cum soluta nobis eleifend

11/14 PT NEUE HELVETICA 55 ROMAN

UT WISI ENIM AD MINIM VENIAM, QUIS NOSTRUD EXERCI TATION ullamcorper suscipit lobortis nisl ut aliquip ex ea commodo consequat. Duis autem vel eum iriure dolor in hendrerit in vulputate velit esse molestie consequat, vel illum dolore eu feugiat nulla facilisis at vero eros et accumsan et iusto odio dignissim qui blandit praesent luptatum zzril

Neue Helvetica 56 Italic

abcdefghijklmnopqrstuvwxyz 1234567890
ABCDEFGHIJKLMNOPQRSTUVWXYZ

Neue Helvetica 65 Medium

abcdefghijklmnopqrstuvwxyz 1234567890
ABCDEFGHIJKLMNOPQRSTUVWXYZ

Neue Helvetica 75 Bold

abcdefghijklmnopqrstuvwxyz 1234567890
ABCDEFGHIJKLMNOPQRSTUVWXYZ

Neue Helvetica 85 Heavy

abcdefghijklmnopqrstuvwxyz
1234567890 ABCDEFGHIJKLMNOPQRST

Neue Helvetica 95 Black

abcdefghijklmnopqrstuvwxyz
1234567890 ABCDEFGHIJKLMNOPQRS

Neue Helvetica 55 Roman

abcdefghijklm
nopqrstuvwxyz
ABCDEFGHIJKLM
NOPQRSTUVWXYZ
1234567890 ¼ ½ ¾
[àóüßç](.,:;?!$€£&-*)
{ÀÓÜÇ}

OPTIMA

TYPE DESIGNER: Hermann Zapf ¶ **FIRST APPEARANCE:** 1958
CLASSIFICATION: Humanist Sans

USE FOR: Pharmaceutical and beauty packaging, religious publications

Like certain other typefaces featured in this book, Optima is a little tricky to classify. It has Glyphic qualities, like characters cut from stone, and it has been said that the designer Hermann Zapf's inspiration for the face came during a visit to the *Basilica di Santa Croce* in Florence when he observed names carved into the gravestones on the church floor. However, Zapf was a master calligrapher and the evidence of his skill can be seen in every stroke of Optima, making it a Humanist Sans. He began working on the face in 1952 and named it Neu Antiqua, but when the Stempel Type Foundry released it in 1958 they switched to Optima, a change which the modest Zapf apparently found embarrassing as he felt it was too grandiose a name. It's a beautiful typeface and instantly recognisable, as there are few others with its singular qualities. The 2002 version Optima Nova, a collaboration between Zapf and Akira Kobayashi, offers a raft of improvements over previous digital releases.

KEY FEATURES FOR CLASSIFICATION AND IDENTIFICATION

- High contrast with a moderate x-height
- Near vertical stress
- Straight strokes are flared at terminals
- Terminals are cupped

8/11 PT OPTIMA ROMAN

LOREM IPSUM DOLOR SIT AMET, CONSECTETUER ADIPISCING ELIT, SED DIAM NONUMMY NIBH euismod tincidunt ut laoreet dolore magna aliquam erat volutpat. Ut wisi enim ad minim veniam, quis nostrud exerci tation ullamcorper suscipit lobortis nisl ut aliquip ex ea commodo consequat. Duis autem vel eum iriure dolor in hendrerit in vulputate velit esse molestie consequat, vel illum dolore eu feugiat nulla facilisis at vsero eros et accumsan et iusto odio dignissim qui blandit praesent luptatum zzril delenit augue duis dolore te feugait nulla facilisi. Nam liber tempor cum soluta nobis eleifend option congue nihil

11/14 PT OPTIMA ROMAN

UT WISI ENIM AD MINIM VENIAM, QUIS NOSTRUD EXERCI TATION ullamcorper suscipit lobortis nisl ut aliquip ex ea commodo consequat. Duis autem vel eum iriure dolor in hendrerit in vulputate velit esse molestie consequat, vel illum dolore eu feugiat nulla facilisis at vero eros et accumsan et iusto odio dignissim qui blandit praesent luptatum zzril

Optima Italic

abcdefghijklmnopqrstuvwxyz 1234567890
ABCDEFGHIJKLMNOPQRSTUVWXYZ

Optima Medium

abcdefghijklmnopqrstuvwxyz 1234567890
ABCDEFGHIJKLMNOPQRSTUVWXYZ

Optima Demi

abcdefghijklmnopqrstuvwxyz 1234567890
ABCDEFGHIJKLMNOPQRSTUVWXYZ

Optima Bold

abcdefghijklmnopqrstuvwxyz 1234567890
ABCDEFGHIJKLMNOPQRSTUVWXYZ

Optima Black

abcdefghijklmnopqrstuvwxyz 1234567890
ABCDEFGHIJKLMNOPQRSTUVWXYZ

Optima Roman

abcdefghijklm
nopqrstuvwxyz
ABCDEFGHIJKLM
NOPQRSTUVWXYZ
1234567890 ¼ ½ ¾
[àóüßç](.,:;?!$€£&-*)
{ÀÓÜÇ}

ITC AVANT GARDE GOTHIC

TYPE DESIGNERS: Herb Lubalin and Tom Carnase ¶ **FIRST APPEARANCE:** 1970
CLASSIFICATION: Geometric Sans

USE FOR: Very tightly spaced headlines with a 1970s flavour

The first commercial release by the International Typeface Corporation, ITC Avant Garde takes its inspiration from the logo of the late 1960s cultural magazine *Avant Garde*, which ITC founding partner Herb Lubalin art directed. The logo was drawn by Lubalin's design partner Tom Carnase. After the need for a typeface to use on promotional material was identified, ITC Avant Garde Gothic was produced as a display font for sole use by the magazine. However, public demand persuaded ITC to develop the face into a full commercial family with additional weights and lowercase characters for text setting. The face is notorious for its misuse; the plethora of complex ligatures and the option to space characters very tightly meant that well-meaning designers managed to produce some fairly hideous typography with it during the 1970s, but it remains a key typeface of the period. Having fallen out of favour, this unmistakable typeface has experienced a renewed surge in popularity in recent years.

KEY FEATURES FOR CLASSIFICATION AND IDENTIFICATION

- Zero contrast with very large x-height
- Vertical stress
- Round glyphs are perfect circles
- 'R' has an open bowl (which is closed for the heavier weights)

166

8/11 PT ITC AVANT GARDE GOTHIC BOOK

LOREM IPSUM DOLOR SIT AMET, CONSECTETUER ADIPISCING ELIT, SED DIAM NONUMMY NIBH euismod tincidunt ut laoreet dolore magna aliquam erat volutpat. Ut wisi enim ad minim veniam, quis nostrud exerci tation ullamcorper suscipit lobortis nisl ut aliquip ex ea commodo consequat. Duis autem vel eum iriure dolor in hendrerit in vulputate velit esse molestie consequat, vel illum dolore eu feugiat nulla facilisis at vsero eros et accumsan et iusto odio dignissim qui blandit praesent luptatum zzril delenit augue duis dolore te feugait nulla facilisi. Nam liber

11/14 PT ITC AVANT GARDE GOTHIC BOOK

UT WISI ENIM AD MINIM VENIAM, QUIS NOSTRUD EXERCI tation ullamcorper suscipit lobortis nisl ut aliquip ex ea commodo consequat. Duis autem vel eum iriure dolor in hendrerit in vulputate velit esse molestie consequat, vel illum dolore eu feugiat nulla facilisis at vero eros et accumsan et iusto odio dignissim qui blandit

ITC Avant Garde Gothic Extra Light

abcdefghijklmnopqrstuvwxyz 1234567890
ABCDEFGHIJKLMNOPQRSTUVWXYZ

ITC Avant Garde Gothic Book Oblique

abcdefghijklmnopqrstuvwxyz 1234567890
ABCDEFGHIJKLMNOPQRSTUVWXYZ

ITC Avant Garde Gothic Medium

abcdefghijklmnopqrstuvwxyz 1234567890
ABCDEFGHIJKLMNOPQRSTUVWXYZ

ITC Avant Garde Gothic Demi

abcdefghijklmnopqrstuvwxyz 1234567890
ABCDEFGHIJKLMNOPQRSTUVWXYZ

ITC Avant Garde Selected Ligatures

CA CO CO EA FA FR GA GO HT CK AL AM MN NT CC
RR RA SS ST TH TU TV VW

ITC Avant Garde Gothic

abcdefghijklm
nopqrstuvwxyz
ABCDEFGHIJKLM
NOPQRSTUVWXYZ
1234567890 ¼ ½ ¾
(àóüßç)(.,:;?!$€£&-*)
{ÀÓÜÇ}

FRUTIGER

TYPE DESIGNER: Adrian Frutiger ¶ **FIRST APPEARANCE:** 1974–1976
CLASSIFICATION: Humanist Sans

USE FOR: Signage systems with type appearing in a large range of sizes

Before its release as a commercial typeface, Frutiger had a different name: Roissy. This stems from the location of Paris Charles de Gaulle airport, the construction of which began in 1966. The prolific French designer Adrian Frutiger was commissioned to design a new typeface for the airport's signage system in 1968 (having previously worked on signage for the Paris Metro) and drew his inspiration from several typefaces; his own Univers, Gill Sans and Edward Johnston's London Underground face. The result, which was renamed Frutiger after its commercial release as an augmented family by Linotype in 1976, is to this day considered to be one of the best faces available for legible signage. There are a couple of contemporary updates available, both of which were overseen by Frutiger. Frutiger Next (1999) has a slightly larger x-height, taller ascenders and true cursive italics. Neue Frutiger (2009 with Akira Kobayashi) reintroduces sloped roman italics alongside a range of optical improvements.

KEY FEATURES FOR CLASSIFICATION AND IDENTIFICATION

- Minimal contrast with a large x-height
- Vertical stress
- Dots are square
- Outward-facing strokes shear off vertically at the terminals

8/11 PT FRUTIGER 55 ROMAN

LOREM IPSUM DOLOR SIT AMET, CONSECTETUER ADIPISCING ELIT, SED DIAM NONUMMY NIBH euismod tincidunt ut laoreet dolore magna aliquam erat volutpat. Ut wisi enim ad minim veniam, quis nostrud exerci tation ullamcorper suscipit lobortis nisl ut aliquip ex ea commodo consequat. Duis autem vel eum iriure dolor in hendrerit in vulputate velit esse molestie consequat, vel illum dolore eu feugiat nulla facilisis at vsero eros et accumsan et iusto odio dignissim qui blandit praesent luptatum zzril delenit augue duis dolore te feugait nulla facilisi. Nam liber tempor cum

11/14 PT FRUTIGER 55 ROMAN

UT WISI ENIM AD MINIM VENIAM, QUIS NOSTRUD EXERCI TATION ullamcorper suscipit lobortis nisl ut aliquip ex ea commodo consequat. Duis autem vel eum iriure dolor in hendrerit in vulputate velit esse molestie consequat, vel illum dolore eu feugiat nulla facilisis at vero eros et accumsan et iusto odio dignissim qui blandit

FRUTIGER 45 LIGHT

abcdefghijklmnopqrstuvwxyz 1234567890
ABCDEFGHIJKLMNOPQRSTUVWXYZ

FRUTIGER 56 ITALIC

abcdefghijklmnopqrstuvwxyz 1234567890
ABCDEFGHIJKLMNOPQRSTUVWXYZ

FRUTIGER 65 BOLD

abcdefghijklmnopqrstuvwxyz 1234567890
ABCDEFGHIJKLMNOPQRSTUVWXYZ

FRUTIGER 75 BLACK

abcdefghijklmnopqrstuvwxyz
1234567890 ABCDEFGHIJKLMNOPQRSTU

FRUTIGER 95 ULTRA BLACK

abcdefghijklmnopqrstuvwxyz
1234567890 ABCDEFGHIJKLMNOPQR

FRUTIGER 55 ROMAN

abcdefghijklm
nopqrstuvwxyz
ABCDEFGHIJKLM
NOPQRSTUVWXYZ
1234567890 ¼ ½ ¾
[àóüßç](.,:;?!$€£&-*)
{ÀÓÜÇ}

AVENIR

TYPE DESIGNER: Adrian Frutiger ¶ **FIRST APPEARANCE:** 1988
CLASSIFICATION: Geometric Sans

USE FOR: Highly legible geometric typography

Avenir was designed by the late Adrian Frutiger and is his Futura. That's not to say for a second that it's a Futura revival – far from it – but Frutiger himself is on record as stating that, 'Right from the beginning, I was convinced that Avenir is the better Futura.' It was designed approximately sixty years after Futura and released in 1988, and Frutiger was able to draw on a wealth of experience and of course new technology to help solve some of the inherent legibility issues caused by Futura's perfect geometry. Unmodulated stroke widths are dropped in favour of a minimal amount of contrast, and perfect circles give way to gracefully modulated curves. Character widths are more harmonious overall and the x-height is a little larger. Also the switch from a single- to double-storey 'a' is significant and provides a helpful identifier. These changes all help to produce a Geometric Sans which is more legible when set at smaller point sizes and is in many ways a warmer, more approachable prospect than its inspirational source.

KEY FEATURES FOR CLASSIFICATION AND IDENTIFICATION

- Minimal contrast with a moderate x-height
- Vertical stress
- Round glyphs are circular
- 'Q' has flat tail aligned to the baseline

8/11 PT AVENIR 45 BOOK

LOREM IPSUM DOLOR SIT AMET, CONSECTETUER ADIPISCING ELIT, SED DIAM NONUMMY NIBH euismod tincidunt ut laoreet dolore magna aliquam erat volutpat. Ut wisi enim ad minim veniam, quis nostrud exerci tation ullamcorper suscipit lobortis nisl ut aliquip ex ea commodo consequat. Duis autem vel eum iriure dolor in hendrerit in vulputate velit esse molestie consequat, vel illum dolore eu feugiat nulla facilisis at vsero eros et accumsan et iusto odio dignissim qui blandit praesent luptatum zzril delenit augue duis dolore te feugait nulla facilisi. Nam liber tempor cum soluta nobis eleifend

11/14 PT AVENIR 45 BOOK

UT WISI ENIM AD MINIM VENIAM, QUIS NOSTRUD EXERCI TATION ullamcorper suscipit lobortis nisl ut aliquip ex ea commodo consequat. Duis autem vel eum iriure dolor in hendrerit in vulputate velit esse molestie consequat, vel illum dolore eu feugiat nulla facilisis at vero eros et accumsan et iusto odio dignissim qui blandit praesent luptatum

Avenir 35 Light

abcdefghijklmnopqrstuvwxyz 1234567890
ABCDEFGHIJKLMNOPQRSTUVWXYZ

Avenir 45 Book Oblique

abcdefghijklmnopqrstuvwxyz 1234567890
ABCDEFGHIJKLMNOPQRSTUVWXYZ

Avenir 55 Roman

abcdefghijklmnopqrstuvwxyz 1234567890
ABCDEFGHIJKLMNOPQRSTUVWXYZ

Avenir 85 Heavy

abcdefghijklmnopqrstuvwxyz 1234567890
ABCDEFGHIJKLMNOPQRSTUVWXYZ

Avenir 95 Black

abcdefghijklmnopqrstuvwxyz 1234567890
ABCDEFGHIJKLMNOPQRSTUVWXYZ

Avenir 45 Book

abcdefghijklm
nopqrstuvwxyz
ABCDEFGHIJKLM
NOPQRSTUVWXYZ
1234567890 ¼ ½ ¾
[àóüßç](.,:;?!$€£&-*)
{ÀÓÜÇ}

ITC OFFICINA SANS

TYPE DESIGNER: Erik Spiekermann and Ole Schäfer
FIRST APPEARANCE: 1990 ¶ **CLASSIFICATION:** Neo-Humanist Sans

USE FOR: Business-like text printed on low-grade paper stock

Erik Spiekermann designed the first two weights of ITC Officina in 1988 under the working name ITC Correspondence. He used the monospaced fonts Letter Gothic and Courier as points of reference and created a more elegant Neo-Humanist Sans that would retain its legibility when printed on the low-quality laser printers available in the late 1980s and 1990s. Output quality was poor compared to that which we're used to today. There are some neat and subtle touches built into the design of the letterforms; angled terminals add personality without compromising legibility, and the corners of the strokes have a tiny amount of roundness in a nod to the impressions left by a mechanical typewriter. Following its broad and favourable acceptance by the design community, the ITC Officina Sans family (and its companion family, ITC Officina Serif) were enlarged by Spiekermann's colleague Ole Schäfer to include five weights, all with an accompanying italic style.

KEY FEATURES FOR CLASSIFICATION AND IDENTIFICATION

- Low contrast with fairly large x-height
- Vertical contrast
- Strokes have angled terminals
- Stroke corners are rounded off

8/11 PT ITC OFFICINA SANS BOOK

LOREM IPSUM DOLOR SIT AMET, CONSECTETUER ADIPISCING ELIT, SED DIAM NONUMMY NIBH EUISMOD TINCIDUNT UT laoreet dolore magna aliquam erat volutpat. Ut wisi enim ad minim veniam, quis nostrud exerci tation ullamcorper suscipit lobortis nisl ut aliquip ex ea commodo consequat. Duis autem vel eum iriure dolor in hendrerit in vulputate velit esse molestie consequat, vel illum dolore eu feugiat nulla facilisis at vsero eros et accumsan et iusto odio dignissim qui blandit praesent luptatum zzril delenit augue duis dolore te feugait nulla facilisi. Nam liber tempor cum soluta nobis eleifend option congue nihil imperdiet doming id quod mazim placerat facer possim assum.

11/14 PT ITC OFFICINA SANS BOOK

UT WISI ENIM AD MINIM VENIAM, QUIS NOSTRUD EXERCI TATION ULLAMCORPER SUSCIPIT lobortis nisl ut aliquip ex ea commodo consequat. Duis autem vel eum iriure dolor in hendrerit in vulputate velit esse molestie consequat, vel illum dolore eu feugiat nulla facilisis at vero eros et accumsan et iusto odio dignissim qui blandit praesent luptatum zzril delenit augue duis dolore te feugait nulla facilisi. Nam liber tempor

ITC Officina Sans Book Italic

abcdefghijklmnopqrstuvwxyz 1234567890
ABCDEFGHIJKLMNOPQRSTUVWXYZ

ITC Officina Sans Medium

abcdefghijklmnopqrstuvwxyz 1234567890
ABCDEFGHIJKLMNOPQRSTUVWXYZ

ITC Officina Sans Bold

abcdefghijklmnopqrstuvwxyz 1234567890
ABCDEFGHIJKLMNOPQRSTUVWXYZ

ITC Officina Extra Bold

abcdefghijklmnopqrstuvwxyz 1234567890
ABCDEFGHIJKLMNOPQRSTUVWXYZ

ITC Officina Sans Black

abcdefghijklmnopqrstuvwxyz 1234567890
ABCDEFGHIJKLMNOPQRSTUVWXYZ

ITC Officina Sans Book

abcdefghijklm
nopqrstuvwxyz
ABCDEFGHIJKLM
NOPQRSTUVWXYZ
1234567890 ¼ ½ ¾
[àóüßç](.,:;?!$€£&-*)
{ÀÓÜÇ}

GOTHAM

TYPE DESIGNER: Tobias Frere-Jones ¶ **FIRST APPEARANCE:** 2000
CLASSIFICATION: Geometric Sans

USE FOR: Forthright typography that means what it says

Gotham is one of those typefaces, like Helvetica, that somehow inveigles itself into the public's consciousness. It has been said that, while most Geometric Sans faces have a distinct German or Swiss flavour, Gotham feels American. This could be put down to its exposure as the typeface used for Barack Obama's 2008 presidential campaign publicity material, but it was already a popular face in the US and elsewhere by then, so who knows? There's something about this face that feels reliable and solid, which may be explained by its source of inspiration. Tobias Frere-Jones, who at the time was part of the Hoefler & Frere-Jones digital type foundry, took the signage above the Eighth Avenue Port Authority Bus Terminal as his point of reference in answer to a commission for a new 'masculine' sans serif for *GQ* magazine. The result is a typeface that is among the most important to be released in the last fifty years. Use the 'M', with its raised vertex, or the unusually tall 't' to spot this face.

KEY FEATURES FOR CLASSIFICATION AND IDENTIFICATION

- Minimal contrast with a large x-height
- Vertical stress
- Vertex of 'M' sits far above the baseline
- Bar of the 't' sits far to the right

8/11 PT GOTHAM BOOK

LOREM IPSUM DOLOR SIT AMET, CONSECTETUER ADIPISCING ELIT, SED DIAM NONUMMY NIBH euismod tincidunt ut laoreet dolore magna aliquam erat volutpat. Ut wisi enim ad minim veniam, quis nostrud exerci tation ullamcorper suscipit lobortis nisl ut aliquip ex ea commodo consequat. Duis autem vel eum iriure dolor in hendrerit in vulputate velit esse molestie consequat, vel illum dolore eu feugiat nulla facilisis at vsero eros et accumsan et iusto odio dignissim qui blandit praesent luptatum zzril delenit augue duis dolore te feugait nulla

11/14 PT GOTHAM BOOK

UT WISI ENIM AD MINIM VENIAM, QUIS NOSTRUD EXERCI tation ullamcorper suscipit lobortis nisl ut aliquip ex ea commodo consequat. Duis autem vel eum iriure dolor in hendrerit in vulputate velit esse molestie consequat, vel illum dolore eu feugiat nulla facilisis at vero eros et accumsan et iusto odio

GOTHAM LIGHT

abcdefghijklmnopqrstuvwxyz 1234567890
ABCDEFGHIJKLMNOPQRSTUVWXYZ

GOTHAM BOOK ITALIC

abcdefghijklmnopqrstuvwxyz 1234567890
ABCDEFGHIJKLMNOPQRSTUVWXYZ

GOTHAM MEDIUM

abcdefghijklmnopqrstuvwxyz
1234567890 ABCDEFGHIJKLMNOPQRST

GOTHAM BOLD

abcdefghijklmnopqrstuvwxyz
1234567890 ABCDEFGHIJKLMNOPQRS

GOTHAM BLACK

abcdefghijklmnopqrstuvwxyz
1234567890 ABCDEFGHIJKLMNOPQRST

GOTHAM BOOK

abcdefghijklm
nopqrstuvwxyz
ABCDEFGHIJKLM
NOPQRSTUVWXYZ
1234567890 ¼ ½ ¾
[àóüßç](.,:;?!$€£&-*)
{ÀÓÜÇ}

COOPER BLACK

TYPE DESIGNER: Oswald B. Cooper ¶ **FIRST APPEARANCE:** 1922
CLASSIFICATION: Display

USE FOR: Club-night posters and record covers

Cooper Black is a curiously timeless typeface; throughout the twentieth and twenty-first centuries there are various periods when it was definitely not fashionable (Swiss Style it isn't) but it seems to just keep coming back. Oswald Cooper designed it for the Chicago-based Barnhart Brothers & Spindler Type Foundry in 1922 and its impact was immediate. It wasn't like anything else available at the time and is now regarded as the first 'super-bold' typeface of the twentieth century. BB&S came up with a neat marketing slogan for it, calling it 'the selling type supreme, the multibillionaire sales type'. Cooper had his own slogan, stating that it was 'for far-sighted printers with near-sighted customers'. It was very successful, a bestseller for many years, and by 1926 an italic style had been added. Today its highest profile use is probably the airline easyJet's bold orange logo, but a whole new generation of graphic designers have embraced it anew and it's as popular as ever.

KEY FEATURES FOR CLASSIFICATION AND IDENTIFICATION

- Low contrast with moderate x-height
- Angled stress
- Enormous 'blurred' serifs
- All junctions are bracketed to various degrees

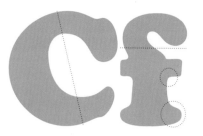

176

18PT COOPER BLACK

QFGbc

36PT COOPER BLACK

QFGbc

72PT COOPER BLACK

QFGbc

Cooper Black Italic

abcdefghijklm
nopqrstuvwxyz
1234567890
ABCDEFGHIJ
KLMNOPQRS
TUVWXYZ

Cooper Black

abcdefghijklm
nopqrstuvwxyz
ABCDEFGHIJKLM
NOPQRSTUVWXYZ
1234567890 ¼½¾
[àóüßç](.,:;?!$€£&-*)
{ÀÓÜÇ}

ITC BAUHAUS

TYPE DESIGNER: Edward Benguiat and Victor Caruso
FIRST APPEARANCE: 1975 ¶ **CLASSIFICATION:** Display

USE FOR: Evoking Europe in the 1930s, anything Bauhaus related

ITC Bauhaus wasn't designed at the Bauhaus – it's an original typeface created for the International Typeface Corporation by Edward Benguiat and Victor Caruso in 1975. They did, however, take an experimental Geometric Sans named Universal, designed by the Bauhaus lecturer Herbert Bayer in 1925, as their point of reference. ITC Bauhaus is very much an interpretation rather than a revival, particularly given that Universal had no uppercase characters while ITC Bauhaus does. In the 1970s, when typographic sensibilities were quite different, it was often used for text setting but it's a display face, as its designers originally intended it to be. Legibility at small point sizes is not this typeface's strong point. It's a fun typeface to use in the right context and its geometric letterforms are instantly recognisable. If you're interested in Bayer's original Universal font, you can purchase an accurate interpretation from the P22 type foundry named P22 Bayer Universal.

KEY FEATURES FOR CLASSIFICATION AND IDENTIFICATION

- Zero contrast with moderate x-height
- Vertical stress
- Many glyphs have open bowls
- Round glyphs are circular

18PT ITC BAUHAUS MEDIUM

BQRxekp

36PT ITC BAUHAUS MEDIUM

BQRxekp

72PT ITC BAUHAUS MEDIUM

BQRxekp

ITC Bauhaus Light

abcdefghijklmnopqrstuvwxyz 1234567890
ABCDEFGHIJKLMNOPQRSTUVWXYZ

ITC Bauhaus Demi

abcdefghijklmnopqrstuvwxyz 1234567890
ABCDEFGHIJKLMNOPQRSTUVWXYZ

ITC Bauhaus Bold

abcdefghijklmnopqrstuvwxyz 1234567890
ABCDEFGHIJKLMNOPQRSTUVWXYZ

ITC Bauhaus Heavy

abcdefghijklmnopqrstuvwxyz 1234567890
ABCDEFGHIJKLMNOPQRSTUVWXYZ

ITC Bauhaus Medium

abcdefghijklm
nopqrstuvwxyz
ABCDEFGHIJKLM
NOPQRSTUVWXYZ
1234567890 ¼ ½ ¾
[àóüßç](.,:;?!$€£&-*)
{ÀÓÜÇ}

TRAJAN

TYPE DESIGNER: Carol Twombly ¶ **FIRST APPEARANCE:** 1989
CLASSIFICATION: Glyphic/Display

USE FOR: Dramatic announcements, movie posters, book covers

If you want to find an example of Trajan in use, look at any blockbuster movie poster and there's a good chance it'll be there. Its statuesque capitals evoke a strong sense of drama that few other glyphic display faces can match. It's very much a display face as there are no lowercase characters, just small caps, and its glyphic qualities stem from the fact that it's modelled closely on the inscriptional characters found at the base of Trajan's Column, a second-century triumphal column in Rome. It's a genuine pioneer typeface as one of the earliest to be designed solely for the digital platform; it was created for the Adobe Originals programme by Carol Twombly in 1989. The original family consisted of just two weights but the latest version, Trajan 3, has six weights ranging from extra light to black. There's now also a corresponding Trajan Sans family with the same six weights.

KEY FEATURES FOR CLASSIFICATION AND IDENTIFICATION
- Moderate contrast with a very large x-height
- Steeply angled stress
- Sharp, asymmetrical serifs
- Open bowls on some glyphs

18PT TRAJAN 3 REGULAR

SARQO

36PT TRAJAN 3 REGULAR

SARQO

72PT TRAJAN 3 REGULAR

Trajan 3 Extra Light
ABCDEFGHIJKLMNOPQRSTUVWXYZ
1234567890 ABCDEFGHIJKLMNOPQRSTU

Trajan 3 Light
ABCDEFGHIJKLMNOPQRSTUVWXYZ
1234567890 ABCDEFGHIJKLMNOPQRST

Trajan 3 Semibold
ABCDEFGHIJKLMNOPQRSTUVWXYZ
1234567890 ABCDEFGHIJKLMNOPQRS

Trajan 3 Bold
ABCDEFGHIJKLMNOPQRSTUVWXYZ
1234567890 ABCDEFGHIJKLMNOPQ

Trajan 3 Black
ABCDEFGHIJKLMNOPQRSTUVWXYZ
1234567890 ABCDEFGHIJKLMNO

Trajan 3 Regular
ABCDEFGHIJKLM
NOPQRSTUVWXYZ
ABCDEFGHIJKLM
NOPQRSTUVWXYZ
1234567890 ¼ ½ ¾
[ÀÓÜßÇ](.,:;?!$€£&-*)
{ÀÓÜÇ}

LUST

TYPE DESIGNER: Neil Summerour ¶ **FIRST APPEARANCE:** 2012
CLASSIFICATION: Display

USE FOR: Vivacious magazine headlines, fashion and grooming products

If Lust were an animal it would be something like a peacock wearing a feather boa for extra effect. Neil Summerour of digital type foundry Positype designed the original Lust typeface family in 2012, and it certainly lives up to its name. It's a wonderfully over-the-top homage to the Rational Serifs or Didones that were so popular in the 1970s, and it clearly takes some of its inspiration from Herb Lubalin's work at the International Typeface Corporation and elsewhere. However, Lust is a different proposal altogether, a very contemporary take on an otherwise familiar style with just enough restraint to keep it legible and, perhaps more importantly, useful – it's perfect for all kinds of editorial applications, and it looks spectacular when set even larger on a poster. As well as the Display variant, the larger family contains regular weights with italic styles, a condensed weight and a script. Look out for the alternative swash and titling glyphs when spotting this typeface, and for the newly released Lust Pro family.

KEY FEATURES FOR CLASSIFICATION AND IDENTIFICATION

- Very high contrast with a fairly large x-height
- Vertical stress
- Extremely fine bracketed serifs
- Hairline strokes meet at most junctions

18PT LUST DISPLAY REGULAR

RAfg71

36PT LUST DISPLAY REGULAR

RAfg71

72PT LUST DISPLAY REGULAR

Lust Display Italic

abcdefghijklmnopqrs
tuvwxyz 1234567890
ABCDEFGHIJK LM
NOPQRSTUVWXYZ

Lust Display Didone

abcdefghijklmnopqrs
tuvwxyz 1234567890
ABCDEFGHIJK LM
NOPQRSTUVWXYZ

Lust Display Regular

abcdefghijklm
nopqrstuvwxyz
ABCDEFGHIJKLM
NOPQRSTUVWXYZ
1234567890 1/4 1/2 3/4
[àóüßç]|(.,:;?!$C£&–*)
{ÀÓÜÇ}

LULO

Type designer: Ryan Martinson ¶ **First appearance:** 2014
Classification: Display

Use for: Evoking an antiquarian feel, replicating woodblock printing

Lulo, a 2014 release by Ryan Martinson of the digital foundry Yellow Design Studio, is an example of the new breed of chromatic typefaces that have appeared in increasing numbers during the last few years. Chromatic fonts (see page 63) are layered typeface families that can be combined to create characters with more than one colour or texture. All one has to do is input text using one of the standard fonts in the package, duplicate the container so it's aligned both horizontally and vertically with the original, and apply an alternative style from those that make up the family. Lulo, a textured typeface that emulates woodblock printing (a specialism of Yellow Design Studio) comes with several options for creating a coloured drop shadow, plus an outline, all of which can be layered up to produce beautiful and, most importantly, fully-editable results. Experimentation is of course key when using chromatic fonts, but the number of effects one can achieve with only a few separate style options is impressive.

Key Features for Classification and Identification

- Minimal contrast with no lower case
- Vertical stress
- Texture emulates letterpress printing
- Round glyphs are circular

18PT LULO BOLD ONE, THREE AND OUTLINE

36PT LULO BOLD ONE, THREE AND OUTLINE

72PT LULO BOLD ONE, THREE AND OUTLINE

Lulo One

ABCDEFGHIJKLMNOPQRST
UVWXYZ 1234567890

Lulo Two

ABCDEFGHIJKLMNOPQRST
UVWXYZ 1234567890

Lulo Three

ABCDEFGHIJKLMNOPQRST
UVWXYZ 1234567890

Lulo Four

ABCDEFGHIJKLMNOPQRST
UVWXYZ 1234567890

Lulo Outline

ABCDEFGHIJKLMNOPQRST
UVWXYZ 1234567890

Lulo One and Two

ABCDEFGH
IJKLMNOPQR
STUVWXYZ
1234567890
¼ ½ ¾ [ÀÓÜßÇ]
(. , : ; ?!$€£&-*)
{ÀÓÜÇ}

USEFUL SHORTCUTS

The chart below lists examples of the keystrokes required to access a broad range of characters or glyphs, which do not have a dedicated key on a standard keyboard.

PC: To access the extended character set hold down the ALT key while typing a glyph's corresponding numbers on the keypad (including the preceding zero).

Mac: The glyphs accessible by using the CONTROL key may not work in all applications.

Glyph	PC	Mac	Glyph	PC	Mac	Glyph	PC	Mac
#	⇧-3	alt-3	µ	alt-0181	alt-M	ç	alt-0231	alt-C
~	⇧-`	⇧-`	¶	alt-0182	alt-7	è	alt-0232	alt-`E
€	alt-0128	alt-2	·	alt-0183	⇧-alt-9	é	alt-0233	alt-EE
‚	alt-0130	⇧-alt-0	¸	alt-0184	⇧-alt-Z	ê	alt-0234	alt-IE
ƒ	alt-0131	alt-F	¹	alt-0185	ctrl-W	ë	alt-0235	alt-UE
„	alt-0132	⇧-alt-W	º	alt-0186	alt-0	ì	alt-0236	alt-`I
…	alt-0133	alt-;	»	alt-0187	⇧-alt-\	í	alt-0237	alt-EI
†	alt-0134	alt-T	¼	alt-0188	ctrl-V	î	alt-0238	alt-II
‡	alt-0135	⇧-alt-7	½	alt-0189	ctrl-U	ï	alt-0239	alt-UI
ˆ	alt-0136	⇧-alt-I	¾	alt-0190	ctrl-X	ð	alt-0240	ctrl-B
‰	alt-0137	⇧-alt-E	¿	alt-0191	Control-alt-/	ñ	alt-0241	alt-NN
Š	alt-0138	ctrl-E	À	alt-0192	alt-`⇧-A	ò	alt-0242	alt-`O
‹	alt-0139	⇧-alt-3	Á	alt-0193	⇧-alt-Y	ó	alt-0243	alt-EO
Œ	alt-0140	⇧-alt-Q	Â	alt-0194	⇧-alt-M	ô	alt-0244	alt-IO
Ž	alt-0142	ctrl-N	Ã	alt-0195	alt-N⇧-A	õ	alt-0245	alt-NO
'	alt-0145	alt-]	Ä	alt-0196	alt-U⇧-A	ö	alt-0246	alt-UO
'	alt-0146	⇧-alt-]	Å	alt-0197	⇧-alt-A	÷	alt-0247	alt-/
"	alt-0147	alt-[	Æ	alt-0198	⇧-alt-'	ø	alt-0248	alt-O
"	alt-0148	⇧-alt-[	Ç	alt-0199	⇧-alt-C	ù	alt-0249	alt-`U
•	alt-0149	alt-8	È	alt-0200	alt-`⇧-E	ú	alt-0250	alt-EU
–	alt-0150	alt--	É	alt-0201	alt-E⇧-E	û	alt-0251	alt-IU
—	alt-0151	⇧-alt--	Ê	alt-0202	alt-I⇧-E	ü	alt-0252	alt-UU
˜	alt-0152	⇧-alt-N	Ë	alt-0203	alt-U⇧-E	ý	alt-0253	ctrl-H
™	alt-0153	alt-2	Ì	alt-0204	alt-`⇧-I	þ	alt-0254	ctrl-L
š	alt-0154	ctrl-F	Í	alt-0205	⇧-alt-S	ÿ	alt-0255	alt-UY
›	alt-0155	⇧-alt-4	Î	alt-0206	⇧-alt-D	≠		alt-=
œ	alt-0156	alt-Q	Ï	alt-0207	⇧-alt-F	∞		alt-5
ž	alt-0158	ctrl-O	Ð	alt-0208	ctrl-A	≤		alt-,
Ÿ	alt-0159	alt-U⇧-Y	Ñ	alt-0209	alt-N⇧-N	≥		alt-.
	alt-Space		Ò	alt-0210	⇧-alt-L	∂		alt-D
¡	alt-0161	alt-1	Ó	alt-0211	⇧-alt-H	Σ		alt-W
¢	alt-0162	alt-4	Ô	alt-0212	⇧-alt-J	∏		⇧-alt-P
£	alt-0163	⇧-3	Õ	alt-0213	alt-N⇧-O	π		alt-P
™	alt-0164	⇧-alt-2	Ö	alt-0214	alt-U⇧-O	∫		alt-B
¥	alt-0165	alt-Y	U	alt-0215	ctrl-]	Ω		alt-Z
¦	alt-0166	ctrl-[	Ø	alt-0216	⇧-alt-O	√		alt-V
§	alt-0167	alt-6	Ù	alt-0217	alt-`⇧-U	≈		alt-X
¨	alt-0168	⇧-alt-U	Ú	alt-0218	⇧-alt-;	Δ		alt-J
©	alt-0169	alt-G	Û	alt-0219	alt-I⇧-U	◊		⇧-alt-V
ª	alt-0170	alt-9	Ü	alt-0220	alt-U⇧-U	/		⇧-alt-1
«	alt-0171	alt-\	Ý	alt-0221	ctrl-G	fi		⇧-alt-5
¬	alt-0172	alt-L	Þ	alt-0222	ctrl-K	fl		⇧-alt-6
	alt-0173	ctrl-/	ß	alt-0223	alt-S	ı		⇧-alt-B
®	alt-0174	alt-R	à	alt-0224	alt-`A	˘		⇧-alt-.
¯	alt-0175	⇧-alt-,	á	alt-0225	alt-EA	˙		alt-H
°	alt-0176	⇧-alt-8	â	alt-0226	alt-IA	˚		alt-K
±	alt-0177	Sh-alt-=	ã	alt-0227	alt-NA	˝		⇧-alt-G
²	alt-0178	ctrl-Z	ä	alt-0228	alt-UA	˛		⇧-alt-T
³	alt-0179	ctrl-Y	å	alt-0229	alt-A	ˇ		⇧-alt-X
´	alt-0180	⇧-alt-E	æ	alt-0230	alt-'			

BIBLIOGRAPHY

Blackwell, Lewis. *20th-Century Type*
London: Laurence King Publishing, 2004

Bringhurst, Robert. *The Elements of Typographic Style*
Vancouver: Hartley and Marks Publishers, 2004

Cheng, Karen. *Designing Type*
London: Laurence King Publishing, 2006

Coles, Stephen. *The Geometry of Type: The Anatomy of
100 Essential Typefaces*
London: Thames & Hudson, 2012

Jaspert, W. Pincus; Berry, W. Turner and Johnson,
A. F. *Encyclopaedia of Typefaces*
London: Cassell Illustrated, 2008

Lawson, Alexander. *Anatomy of a Typeface*
New Hampshire: David R. Godine, Inc., 1990

Lupton, Helen. *Thinking With Type (2nd edition)*
New York: Princeton Architectural Press, 2010

McGrew, Mac. *American Metal Typefaces of the
Twentieth Century*
New Rochelle: The Myriade Press, 1986

Seddon, Tony. *The Evolution of Type: A Graphic
Guide to 100 Landmark Typefaces*
London: Thames & Hudson, 2015

INDEX

ACKNOWLEDGEMENTS

I'd like to thank the whole team at RotoVision
for their support during this project; in particular
Isheeta Mustafi for getting me involved in the first
place, Agata Rybicka for creating the original design
concept and for her contributions to the layout and
illustrations, and Abbie Sharman for editorial input
and email wrangling. I'd also like to thank Nick Jones
for handling the editorial side of things, and for his
supportive comments throughout. And of course,
I must once again thank my family and friends,
especially my wife Sarah, for putting up with
a grumpy author who (possibly) spends too much
time staring at typefaces.